D1785429

WOOD TOY MAKING

TOY making in wood is a fascinating occupation, and in this book the author deals with his subject from the viewpoint of the ordinary man in his home workshop.

Details of materials and adhesives, and wheels, are included, and the important aspect of decorative finishing is well covered. A variety of toys are described and illustrated with clear drawings and simple working instructions. To amateur woodworkers who aspire to make wooden toys, this will be really useful.

WOOD TOY MAKING

By

W. A. G. BRADMAN, R.R.S.A.
Member of the Institute of Journalists

Illustrated by the Author

MAGNA PRINT BOOKS
LITTON . YORKSHIRE

First Published in large print 1975
by
Magna Print Books
Litton, Skipton, Yorkshire
by arrangement with
W. & G. Foyle Limited
London

© Large Print Edition 1975
Magna Print Books
ISBN 0 86009 035 3

Printed in Great Britain

CONTENTS

INTRODUCTION

ONE of the most pleasurable woodwork tasks is that of making children's toys. This applied equally whether the toys are intended for the woodworker's own children or are made for profit. The work affords opportunities for introducing personal touches and much ingenuity can be employed to contrive toys of real artistic worth. The art of toy-making is as old as civilisation itself and will continue so long as civilisation lasts. From prehistoric times men have fashioned toys according to the material at their disposal and one of the earliest of these was wood. Its use has continued until the present day.

Wood itself is a remarkable substance, friendly to the touch, easily worked and above all robust in use. It is easily capable of being smoothed and finished so that it is safe and agreeable to tiny hands — points which must never be overlooked.

In this book I have set out to interest you, the reader, in this most fascinating task. Quite obviously it is impossible for me to cover the innumerable varieties of wood toys and I have therefore endeavoured to present a brief selection from the huge field available. It is not my intention that you should be bound to adhere to the precise designs shown, for as I have already said the personal touch is yours alone. I hope you will employ it and treat the designs more as suggestions and references than as rigidly enforced instructions.

One thing I am bound to say — it is important and should never be ignored. Remember always that a child's conception of a particular toy may be markedly different to your own. That which may appear incongruous to the adult mind frequently delights a child and is accepted as perfectly natural. Children regard their toys often with more seriousness than we regard our houses or our cars. At the same time the child lives in a world of fantastic make-believe — a world in which anything can do anything — and frequently does! Also remember, the keynote of this world is simplicity. Intricate detail, complex mechanisms and "last minute" fripperies simply do not belong to the child's world. A strip of wood, pointed at one end and hauled by a string through a puddle

—(preferably a dirty one!)—can be any child's "Queen Elizabeth". Funnels, lifeboats, passengers and even bow wave — all are supplied by courtesy of his imagination!

This does not mean that details should never be included in toy design — on the contrary they should, but it is the logical details that are required. For instance, no boy would accept a motor-car without its steering wheel. It matters not that the "wheel" be a plain disc nailed to a dowel, or that the front wheels do not swivel even if the disc can be rotated. To him a motor car needs a driver (whom he will cheerfully supply in his imagination) — therefore the driver needs a steering wheel, without which the toy is not a motor car!

Other details can of course be included but it is often better to suggest them rather than attempt close detail work which seldom convinces. Thus the motor car could have "headlamps" of white paint or a "radiator" suggested in black.

A final point — remember the child's love of colour but also its sense of fitness. A toy duck can quite easily be blue, pink or almost any colour, provided it is bright and attractive, but a fire-engine must be *red*! Not just any old red, but a full, rich glowing red — the richer the better. It may hit you in the eye every time you see it but it will make him a fireman as soon as he lays hands on it! So with other toys, for the object is to present the child with toys in tune with its world of fantasy and with which he or she will live until time gently and imperceptibly transforms it to the proportions we know so well.

W.A.G.B.

Chapter One

MATERIALS AND ADHESIVES

IN any woodwork project the selection of the particular material to be used plays an important part in the ultimate success or failure of the job. Wood toys are no exception to the rule, but somehow its importance tends often to be forgotten, particularly when the toy is to be painted. First, then, let us consider some of the more commonly available timbers with due regard to their usefulness for toy making.

Natural Timbers

Timbers are divided into two classes, hardwoods and softwoods and these delightfully vague terms at once constitute a trap for the unwary! Thus we find that some "hardwoods" are in the physical sense softer than some "softwoods", and vice versa. The terms are purely botanical distinctions between timber obtained from broad-leaved trees and those with needle shaped leaves.

The broad-leaved trees produce "hardwood" whilst the needle-leaved trees give us "softwood".

The selection of timber for toy making must always be determined by the nature and size of the toy. For instance a tiny "engine" which the child will merely push around the floor could be made of almost any wood, but a larger version which he will certainly want to ride on, needs a robust timber if it is not to collapse after a short period of use.

The most frequently used timber for furniture making is oak, yet in spite of its undoubted strength and hard wearing qualities it is generally unsuitable for toy making. The reason is that oak is a timber which readily absorbs moisture and is well known for its tendency to "move" or shrink and expand with changes in humidity. This produces warping and consequent "loss of shape" in the parts but is not of great moment as the sizes used are relatively small. The real drawback in using oak for toys is its tendency to splinter which makes it dangerous for children's use as these oak splinters are brittle and generally very sharp. If one is run into the finger the fine, needle like points are apt to break as it is withdrawn and the wound is thus painful and prone to festering.

Pine and deal are other unsuitable timbers as they, too, easily split and thus raise similar objections to oak. Suitable timbers, however, are sycamore, mahogany, beech, ash and birch. These woods are close grained and can be used with confidence. Ash is particularly valuable for parts which may be subjected to much strain but it is often difficult to drive screws into this wood. Pre-drilling to the required depth is advisable, also the use of a little candle wax rubbed on the screw threads. (This is always a wise precaution as it makes withdrawal of the screw an easy job and helps to prevent the shank fracturing due to excessive friction as it is driven in.) Mahogany is strictly speaking a "furniture" wood but has been included as it can often be obtained from discarded furniture. Sycamore and birch are more frequently seen nowadays due to the increased use of home grown timbers, whilst beech is perhaps the favourite wood for toymakers due to its hardness and close grain, making it possible to obtain a clean smooth finish with little trouble.

The most usual source of timber supply for wood toys will be off-cuts which can usually be obtained quite cheaply. One will of course need to reduce the wood to width and thickness but providing that a large number of toys are not being constructed at the same time the "conversion" work should not be excessive. It is as well, however, to keep a watch for broken screw shanks, nails, etc., as these may easily gash the plane-iron or possibly break off saw teeth. In general, when using "second-hand" material it should be carefully examined and any holes probed with a needle point. This will immediately reveal a broken-off nail or screw shank and thus avoid damage to cutting edges.

Plywood

Apart from natural timber there are other materials which are suitable for toymaking. The first of these is of course plywood in various thicknesses and laminations. This too is generally available in offcut sizes and is a useful all round material. "Three-ply" is the most widely used variety and is generally strong enough for most toy applications. Two points should be noted when using "three-ply" material. First it generally has a tendency to go hollow if allowed to get wet but this can usually be avoided by sealing the material with a coat of paint or varnish. Secondly, the outer plies are apt to split if anything much thicker than veneer pins are driven into the edge of the sheet. This frequently occurs when making a light box construction. Better fixing methods are either to use through dovetail joints or to employ a small batten at the inside corner and fix by pinning through into this from the outside faces. If the pins themselves are set dovetail fashion the joint is quite strong.

In the case of multiple-ply or blockboard these remarks do not apply with such force although large nails may well split the material. Multiple-ply is generally thicker than three-ply and therefore more able to resist the splitting stresses, whilst blockboard consists of narrow strips of softwood sandwiched between double veneer "skins".

Hardboard

Hardboard is a material extensively used nowadays as an alternative to plywood. It is generally composed of layers of paper compressed into a dense flat sheet, usually 3/16 in. or 1/4 in. thick. Alternatively, wood or paper pulp may be used to make up the sheets and in some cases these are impregnated with resin. Although up to now hardboard has not been greatly used for toy making, it does possess qualities which recommend it, particularly where the toy is to be painted or enamelled. Chief amongst these are its freedom from warping tendencies and the ability to receive nails close to the edge without breaking away.

Usually brown in colour, hardboard can be obtained from most wood stores or builders' yards and is frequently available in offcut sizes. It is strong and can easily be sawn to shape. Edges can be planed smooth but the outer "layers" at each face are liable to "fluff", especially if the plane cutter is not really sharp. The nature of the material tends to dull the cutting edges more rapidly than when used on natural timber. Surface absorption is fairly high and therefore an undercoat is really necessary when finishing with paint or enamel.

Chipboard

Another material of interest to toymakers is chipboard, composed of wood particles impregnated with synthetic resin and compressed into flat boards. Thicknesses range from about 3/8 in.

to 3/4 in. in normal sizes whilst thicker material is sometimes produced. It must be realised that the absence of a regular grain in this material, whilst making it free of warping tendencies, does render the boards less robust than natural timber. It is easily finished with paint or enamel or it may be varnished or french polished. It is a useful material for applications such as walls and roofs of dolls' houses.

Due to the synthetic resins with which chipboard is impregnated, wear on cutting edges is fairly severe. By sawing close to the marking line, the amount of trimming necessary can be kept to a minimum and it is a good plan to occasionally strop the plane cutter on a piece of leather dressed with lubricating oil. If this is done as soon as the edge begins to dull, re-sharpening will not need to be undertaken so often.

One drawback to chipboard is its tendency to break away if nails are placed close to the edge. It is best to drill for nailing and to avoid hammering the nail head after it is flush. A very good purchase is obtained with screws but pre-drilling is necessary. The most suitable adhesives are casein or synthetic glues. Scotch glue does not give a reliable bond.

Dowel Rod

These are available in various sizes from 3/16 in. to 1 in. diameter usually in birch or oak. Lengths vary from about 24 in. to 4 or 5 feet, but dowels can often be obtained "ready made" in lengths of 1 in. to 2 or 2.1/2 in. In these cases the dowels are usually impressed with a spiral groove which allows the glue to escape as the dowel is driven in. After fixing, the dowel absorbs moisture from the glue and swells to grip the wood more tightly. In many cases, dowel rod will be used in toymaking for purposes other than fixing wood parts together. For instance the most obvious application is funnels and masts for toy boats and here as in other applications of this nature, the "plain" dowel rod is obviously the best to use.

ADHESIVES

Scotch Glue

The most commonly used adhesive for wood-work purposes is scotch glue, or, to give its correct title, animal glue. It is, however, surprising how many workers fail to appreciate the simple requirements necessary to obtain good joints with this adhesive. Scotch glue is derived from bones and hide by a surprisingly intricate process which ensures that the glue "cakes", as the familiar slabs of "solid" glue are termed, are pure and of the required consistency.

Upon purchasing glue cake, the first process is to break it into pieces of fairly small size. The method is to wrap the cake in *clean* rag and then to pound it with a mallet. Hammering it on the bench causes it to shatter into fragments which are swept up, together with any dirt, grit or metal particles which are there. Obviously these foreign bodies can easily cause trouble by becoming brushed on to the contact surfaces and thus preventing the close uniform contact which is essential to a good joint.

Following the breaking-up stage, the glue fragments are tipped into the glue-pot and covered with clean water. This is allowed to stand for a day, when the glue cake will have absorbed most of the water and will be jellified. The outer vessel of the glue pot is filled with water and heated until it boils. It is then allowed to simmer for some time until the glue, which is occasionally stirred during the process, forms a frothy scum. This is removed and the simmering continued for a short while to determine that no more scum

19

is produced.

To obtain satisfactory results with scotch glue it should be hot and "thin". Too much heat reduces its tensile strength whilst at the same time a cold glue liquor does not spread well and chills quickly. A good practical test for consistency is to dip the brush into the hot glue, then hold it about six inches above the pot. If the consistency is correct, the glue should run freely off the brush without breaking up into drops.

It is of course obvious that the joints themselves should be well cut, that is to say, they should fit closely together. Scotch glue acts by penetrating the pores of the timber and spreading into the fibres by capillary attraction. Thus between two glued wood surfaces there is a thin membrane, on either side of which the glue has spread into the timber with something like a root formation. So long as this membrane is thin, i.e., the surfaces meet closely, the joint is strong. A joint which "gapes" means a thick glue line which, being brittle, is easily fractured.

A frequent cause of failure can be ascribed to chilled joints. This occurs when hot glue is brushed on to cold wood and allowed to stand before the joints are assembled. Chilling can also be caused by working in a cold atmosphere. The effect is to congeal the glue and thus prevent its ready absorption into the wood fibres. To avoid this fault, work in a warm atmosphere and also warm the contact surfaces immediately before glueing. This is usually done by holding them above a gas ring and keeping the wood moving to avoid it becoming charred.

"Starved" joints are another frequent cause of failure. This occurs where the glue is too thin, through over dilution with water or by overheating the glue. In either case the glue soaks into the wood, leaving the contact surfaces practically dry.

"Cold" Animal Glues

These are animal glues which do not require heating prior to use and therefore have distinct advantages over scotch glue from the aspect of convenience of use. They are packed in tins, jars or tubes and require no mixing processes before use.

The methods of jointing follow normal lines except that warming the contact surfaces is not necessary and the glue, being rather thicker than scotch glue is better handled by spreading with a wooden stick, rather than brushing it on. A convenience which will be appreciated by occasional users is its immediate readiness and economy in use. During very cold weather this type of glue tends to thicken but can easily be brought to working consistency by immersing the container for a short time in warm water. Glue of this type can be had under the following proprietary brands:—

Rawlplug Duroglue. (Manufactured by the Rawlplug Co., Ltd.)

Croid Universal Glue, Croid Aero Glue, Croid Super Glue (Manufactured by Croid Ltd.)

Casein Glue

This is a cold working glue of exceptionally high strength and therefore very suitable for toy making. It is derived from milk curd and also from Soya beans. The casein is ground to a fine powder and mixed with soda and lime and in this form is generally packed in tins or jars. These should be kept well stoppered and stored in a dry place. To prepare the glue it is mixed with cold water to form a creamy liquid.

It is necessary that the correct proportions of powder and water are used, otherwise the glue will be unsuitable. Full directions for mixing are invariably printed on the containers and these should be rigidly followed.

In general, the powder and water are well stirred together for at least five minutes to ensure complete mixing and solution. The liquid is then left to stand for a period of usually fifteen to twenty minutes. It is then ready for use.

This type of glue gradually thickens after mixing, until it becomes unusable. This is called the "pot life" and determines the period during which joints made with the particular mix will prove satisfactory. For this reason only sufficient glue for the job in hand should be made up, but this disadvantage is offset by the ease with which a tiny quantity can be prepared at a time. For instance sufficient casein glue for a single joint can be made by mixing it in an egg-cup, although naturally it saves labour by arranging to mix for a number of joints at one time.

Casein glue has two disadvantages which, whilst not serious, should be mentioned. First it reacts with the tannic acid present in some timbers and thus stains the surface. The depth of stain depends upon the amount of tannic acid present and consequently upon the variety of timber used. Oak is the chief offender in this respect but as it is not a recommended wood for toy making, this disadvantage can be discounted. The second factor to consider is the likelihood of the casein glue setting up skin irritation which occasionally occurs with some people. This too can be avoided by taking due precautions.

Some proprietary brand Casein glues are as follows:—

"Casco" Casein glue (Manufactured by Leicester Lovel & Co.),

"Croid" Casein glue (Manufactured by Croid Ltd.).

Synthetic Resin Adhesives

These glues have been developed in recent years and are widely used in the furniture trade. There are a number of different types, produced for varied purposes, though for bonding wood joints the most commonly used are the Phenol Formaldehyde and Urea Formaldehyde varieties.

In general the adhesives are formed of two separate substances. One of these is the actual resin, a treacly substance which solidifies after some time, and the catalyst or hardener, a liquid which is used to react with the resin and to

24

accelerate its hardening time.

There are two methods of using the adhesive, by mixing and spreading or by separate application. The first method is the more commonly used, the resin and catalyst being mixed in their correct proportions just before use. Pot life is short and only sufficient adhesive to suit the job in hand should be made up at a time. The mixture is spread on the jointing surfaces with a scrap of wood. Using a brush for the purpose is unsuitable as there is no means of cleaning the bristles after use and the brush is thereby ruined.

Separate application technique consists of applying the hardener to one face of the joint and the resin to the other. In certain circumstances this method is used in industry but there is little to commend it for toy making on a restricted scale.

Exceptionally high joint strength is obtained with these adhesives but the necessity for close fitting parts cannot be neglected as the strength is obtained by surface adhesion and not by penetration. Slack joints will therefore only adhere at scattered contact points which naturally greatly reduces the strength of the bond. A properly made joint using correctly mixed

adhesive cannot be separated except by
destruction.

Chapter Two

FITTINGS AND WHEELS

TOY fittings are often regarded much as an afterthought and in many cases the wrong sizes are used or perhaps something is contrived out of the "spare part box". Although improvisation must often be resorted to, it is hardly fair to the worker's own efforts to use makeshifts, when for a small amount of trouble and expense a new and correctly sized part can be used.

Screws

These are perhaps the chief offenders and it is surprising how many good toys are spoilt by the use of wrongly sized or damaged screws. By all means use a "second-hand" screw provided it is in good condition, but do be sure to see that it has no sharp burrs waiting to catch in tiny sensitive fingers.

Also, if the screw has a countersunk head, see that it is really flush in the wood. If it stands proud, the child may easily catch an enquiring fingernail under the sharp edge. A commonly seen fault occurs where countersunk-head screws are used to attach metal fittings to the toy. Close inspection will often show that the countersunk head is not really flush and the remedy is to further countersink the hole or to use a raised head screw if there is sufficient room for the head. This type of screw is really a combination of the round-head and countersunk head types and is often used in conjunction with a brass screw cup. This is employed to increase the bearing surface of the head against the wood and both fittings can be seen in Fig. 1. Wood screw sizes and measurements are points which sometimes confuse woodworkers and it is as well to have a general idea of their significance. Screw sizes are denoted by gauge numbers ranging from 0 to 16 and refer to the *thickness* or *diameter* of the screw shank. Size "o" is the thinnest and the diameter increases with the numbers. The *length* of the screw is always quoted in inches and has no bearing on the gauge number. Thus a 2.1/2 in. No. 8 screw is precisely as thick as a 1/2 in. No. 8 screw, on the other hand a 5/8 in. No. 10 screw is *thicker* than a

2 in. No. 6.

The method of measuring the length of a screw should also be understood. *Countersunk head* screws are measured overall, that is from the flat of the head to the screw point. *Round-head* screws are measured from the *edge* of the screw head to the point of the thread.

The remaining points to bear in mind when ordering screws, especially when obtaining them by post, are the materials of which they are made and any finish desired. In general, two metals are used — brass and iron, so if the required material is not specified you may easily be sent the wrong one. Regarding finishes, iron screws may be nickel plated, chromium plated, black japanned or blued. Brass screws may be nickel plated or chromium plated. In each case, therefore, the finish must be stipulated unless the screws are to be plain finish. There is an accepted manner for ordering screws which it is advisable to follow in order to avoid mistakes. Thus, to obtain "twelve brass wood-screws gauge 8 and 3/4 in. long with chromium plated finish and countersunk heads", they would be ordered as follows:— "1 doz. 3/4 in. No. 8 brass CSK wood screws chromium finish". This tells the shopkeeper all he needs to know, in the accepted manner and he will respect the order as coming from someone who understands exactly what he wants.

Nails

For toy-making the most useful types are ordinary round wire or french nails and oval brads. The latter are not to be confused with shoemakers' brads but are the oval nails shown in Fig. 1. Curiously enough, these are often erroneously referred to as "french nails" when in fact the round wire type are true french nails. Oval brads are generally made in lengths between 3/4 in. and 4 in. and when used are driven in so that the "width" of the nail is in line with the grain. This avoids splitting the wood, particularly when used in thin stuff.

The strength of a nailed joint can sometimes be increased by driving in the nails at a "dovetail" slope. This technique is employed in box making but can be adapted to other uses.

Panel pins are similar to round wire nails but have a smaller and neater head. They range in size from about 1/2 in. to 2 in. long and are a useful means of reinforcing glued joints as the heads are relatively inconspicuous.

Brass pins as their name implies are made of brass and have a rounded head. They range from about 1/2 in. to 1.1/4 in. long and are conveniently used for attaching small straps or fabric to the wood. The brass heads form a neat decoration to the work.

Corrugated fasteners shown in Fig. 1 are a simple and rigid method of fixing joints together. The corrugations converge and thus draw the parts tightly together as the fastener is driven in. They are placed at an angle to the grain, but do not have them too near the edge of the material or it may be sheared away. Care in placing the corrugated fastener is also necessary if it is being used to reinforce a joint. Sometimes a mortise and tenon is not cut quite correctly, and with care a small corrugated fastener can be used to improve matters. The point to watch, however, is that the fastener itself does not shear through the tenon and thus make matters even worse!

Screw eyes are mainly used as a means for attaching towing lines to mobile toys. They are made in brass or iron and can be had in a wide range of sizes. It must be remembered that a screw eye used for towing is subjected to an appreciable strain, so the iron variety is the best to use. Even so, large toys may impose sufficient drag, particularly when the toy is snatched along, to cause the thread to pull out of the wood. In the majority of cases the construction of the toy may call for the screw thread to be driven into end grain, thus raising a similar problem to that discussed later under the sub-heading "Wheels". For towing purposes where larger toys are concerned it is generally better to dispense with the screw eye and to knot a cord through a hole bored in the toy for this purpose. Needless to say, the hole should not be too near the edge or it will probably get broken out in use. It is also a good thing to countersink each side of the hole so that the cord or string does not become frayed on the square edges. Attention to these small points will make all the difference to the lasting qualities of the toy.

Wheels and how they are fixed

In the case of the small toys there are two types of wheels which are used, turned wooden types and the pressed or spun metal patterns. Both kinds are available in several sizes and nowadays they can so easily be obtained that in general it is not worth the trouble of making them,

WOOD TOY MAKING

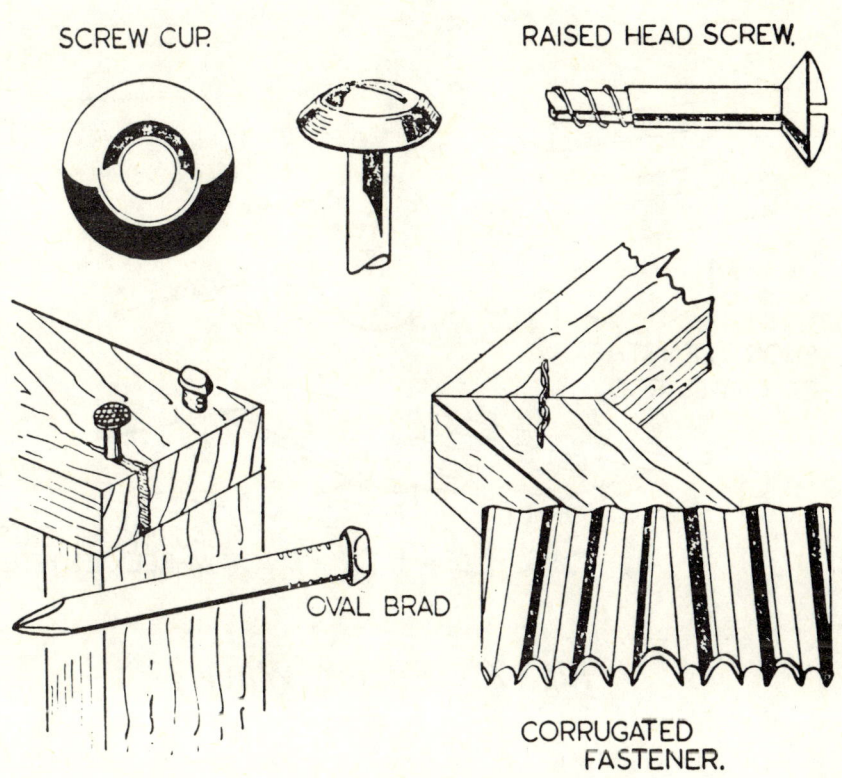

SCREW CUP.

RAISED HEAD SCREW.

OVAL BRAD

CORRUGATED FASTENER.

Fig. 1.   Fixings

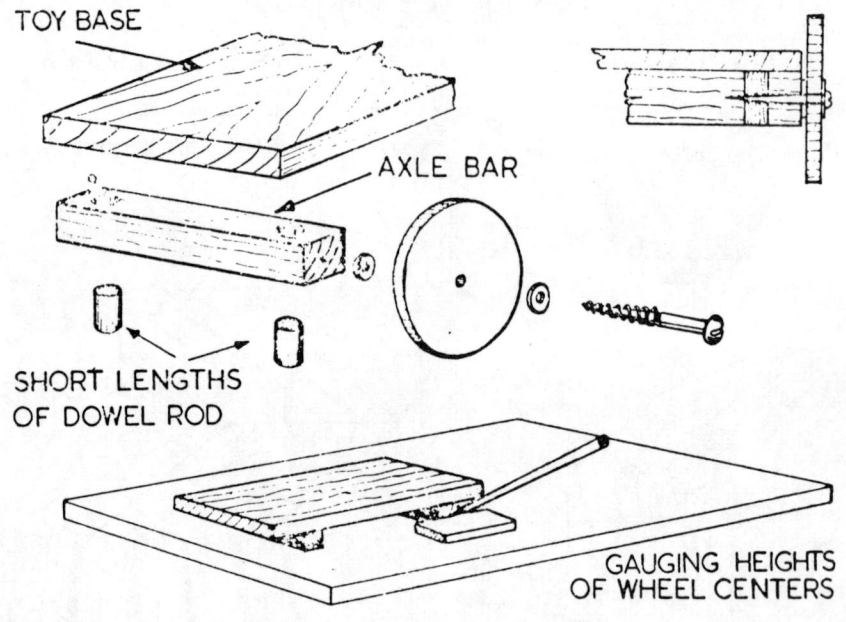

TOY BASE

AXLE BAR

SHORT LENGTHS
OF DOWEL ROD

GAUGING HEIGHTS
OF WHEEL CENTERS

Fig. 2. Fitting Wheels

particularly if the worker does not possess a lathe.

Almost in every case a screw is used for the axle, whichever type of wheel is employed. It is easily the most convenient way of fixing the wheel and provided a little thought is given to the way it is done, the method is perfectly satisfactory.

Wherever possible it is best to avoid driving the axle screw into end grain. This is the weakest method of fixing into wood, as a little thought will show. The screw thread enters the direction of the grain, following down a central hole bores to receive the core of the screw. Unless this hole is bored there is a distinct possibility of splitting the wood yet it aggravates the problem by making it easy for the thread to sever the fibres as the screw is turned. Thus when the screw is fully home the wood fibres immediately surrounding it are chopped into short lengths and the holding power which depends entirely upon the shearing strength of the fibres, is seriously impaired. A very slight over-turning of the screw rips the short fibres from the surrounding timber and the fixing is useless.

In the case of a screw driven into the side of the timber, the position is completely reversed.

If one can imagine the wood greatly enlarged and appearing like a tightly packed bundle of dowel rods to represent the wood fibres lying along the grain, a better impression of the problem is obtained. If a hole is bored into the side of the bundle, some of the dowels will be completely severed whilst others, especially at the top and bottom of the hole, will merely be nicked. When the screw enters the hole the core practically fills it whilst the thread engages the dowels and either packs them more tightly together or runs in the grooves between them. It will now be seen that there is no weakening of the structure and very considerable force is required to pull out the screw without turning it so that the thread disengages.

All this may sound simple and obvious but it is necessary to understand the principles involved in the problem. There will obviously be occasions when screws must be fixed into end grain, particularly in the case of axle screws. You will obviously want to make your toys as robust as possible and to avoid the weakness in these particular cases, some means of reinforcing the fixing is desirable. This, in point of fact, can easily be done as shown in Fig.2. Here the axles are bored through at a short distance from each end and the holes are filled with lengths of dowel rod glued in place. The axle screws engage the dowels and hold firmly in the side grain. It is important that the dowels are not too large or the axle will be weakened. Be sure also to bore a small hole into the dowel for the screw core, otherwise it will certainly split when the screw is driven in. Provision should also be made for spacing washers as shown in Fig. 2. Somehow or other these are seldom used in wood toys yet they make all the difference to their running qualities. The inner washers prevent the wheels rubbing against the axles or base board, whilst the outer ones increase the bearing surface and tend to minimise wheel wobble.

Having discussed the method of fixing the wheels, let us now examine the problem of placing them correctly in position. The first thing is to ensure that the base of the toy is not "in winding", that is to say, it is reasonably flat and does not rock when laid on a flat board. It is also possible that one or other of the axles may be tapered, which would also produce rocking. These faults can be overcome by packing under the "high" corners, until the whole thing stands firmly and then marking the axle positions. It is, however, always best to ensure that the parts are true in the first place.

To ensure that all the axle holes are exactly at the same height a slip of wood is cut and used as a template in the manner shown in Fig. 2. The next point is to square across the base and carry the lines down to meet the height marks. (The importance of having the axle bars fixed squarely across the base will be obvious, otherwise the toy will not run straight.)

Chapter III

FINISHING

THE finishing process is one which should receive most careful attention if the toy is to be successful, or, for that matter if it is to be safe for the youngster to play with. Unfortunately it is a matter which in a distressingly large number of cases is skimped or even completely omitted. From the aesthetic viewpoint alone, it cannot be too strongly emphasised that a good finish on the toy adds immeasurably greater attraction to it and should never be ignored.

There are several different types of finish which may be used and which primarily depend on the actual toy. Whatever type is used, the first consideration is the state of the wood surface. It goes without saying that this should be smooth, clean and free from splinters and a perfunctory rub over with glasspaper is not enough. It may easily roughen after treatment which is obviously unsatisfactory.

At the present day most of the timber we use is machine planed and although free of serious roughness it may not stay in that condition. As the timber passes through the machine, the revolving cutters, in addition to cutting the wood, exert appreciable pressure on its surface. These have the effect of compressing a good deal of the outer fibres into the wood surface which are released if the wood becomes moist at some later date. This results in the rough surface seen on shoddily finished toys, a state to be avoided if they are to be safe or successful.

The cause of this roughness is, of course, the ends of the upstanding fibres which in fact are like a number of tiny splinters. Removal of these fibres is therefore of first importance and should not be ignored.

Scraping

In the long run, the best and easiest way is to cut off the fibres with a cabinet scraper and then to follow with fine grade glasspaper. To do this the wood is deliberately moistened by wiping over with a damp sponge. This releases the compressed fibres which stand up and can then be easily cut off with the scraper.

An efficient form of this tool is the Skarsten Scraper, made by the Skarsten Manufacturing Company. It employs a patented hooked blade held in a specially designed clip and handle, the blade being instantly removable for replacement purposes. The handle provides a positive grip and ensures easy working and the tool can be thoroughly recommended. At the same time there are a number of woodworkers who prefer the ordinary cabinetmaker's scraper which is an extremely efficient tool if sharpened and used properly.

It consists of a piece of cast steel, usually measuring 5 to 6 in. long by 2 in. or so wide. The thickness varies slightly with different makes but is usually of the order of 1/16 in. or so. When choosing a scraper it should be selected for reasonable flexibility whilst at the same time not being too thin. It is held in both hands, the fingers close together and at the back of the scraper whilst the thumbs lie close to each other at the front of the blade and press against the centre. The steel is thus bowed to produce a *very slightly* curved edge. The tool is used by pushing it away from the worker and is held almost square to the grain. In those cases where the size or shape of the wood does not allow sufficient room to scrape with the grain, the blade is held at forty-five degrees and worked straight across the grain. This produces a slicing cut and avoids the tendency for the edge to drop into the soft parts between the "grain" streaks.

About the only difficulty encountered with the cabinet scraper is the process of sharpening, yet this job is very simply done. If the scraper is badly worn, the edge is filed level and square. It is then ground smooth and square, the job being done on the *side* of the oilstone. (The object is to avoid rapid wear on the face of the stone.) If the edge is now felt between finger and thumb, a "wire edge" will be apparent at each side. This has to be removed and is done by laying the scraper flat on the face of the stone and rubbing it round and round. Both sides are treated in this way and the edges are then ready for "turning".

If a properly sharpened scraper is felt, it will be found that the edges present a regular sharp "burr" and it is this feature which actually produces the cut. To form it, the scraper is clamped in the vice and the edge is rubbed with a hard steel tool such as the back of a gouge. Place the gouge at the centre of the edge, square on to the blade and with the tool just less than ninety degrees to the vertical. Stroke evenly and firmly to one corner of the scraper, bring the gouge back to the centre and stroke in the opposite direction. Repeat once or twice, then stroke the whole length of the blade. Reverse the scraper and repeat the process. This "turns over" the corners and forms a minutely hooked cutting edge which is what is required.

Glasspapering

However efficient the scraper is and however carefully the work is done, there are bound to be a few upstanding fibres left and these are dealt with by glasspapering. A good 'finishing" grade is No. "o", though for superfine finishing an even finer glasspaper known as "flour" grade is used.

There is more in glasspapering than merely rubbing over the wood with a sheet of glasspaper. First of all the human hand is not designed to exert an even pressure over a flat surface and in the great majority of cases this is what is required. The correct way to use glasspaper is to wrap it round a block of wood or cork. The work can then be sanded flat without difficulty.

When smoothing down for cabinetmaking special care is always taken to preserve the dead squareness of the edges. In the case of wood toys it is preferable that these should be *very slightly* rounded so that there is no chance of the child cutting a finger on, or picking up a splinter from the edge.

Following the glasspapering stage, the wood is given a thorough dusting and is then ready for the decorative finish.

Painting and Enamelling

Perhaps the most commonly used finish for wood toys is paint or enamel. Properly applied it is hygienic and safe and has much to commend it on aesthetic grounds. The technique is similar in both cases and will therefore be treated as one.

The first coat put on the wood is the primer and its function is to satisfy the natural suction of the wood. Following this is the undercoat which provides opacity and prepares the way for the final or top coat. These three coats are regarded as the minimum required to produce a high class finish and in point of fact, the best work usually receives several more coats. It must, however, be conceded that children's toys do not normally undergo the elaborate coatings of high class finishing and, in fact, except in special cases do not warrant it. The three-coat finish, primer, undercoat and top coat will give excellent results if properly applied.

Primer

A good general purpose primer for wood toys is "Aluminium Wood Primer". It must not be confused with "Aluminium Paint" which is produced for decorative use and is not satisfactory for priming. Aluminium wood primer consists of finely ground aluminium powder suspended in a varnish which is selected mainly for its quality of adhering firmly to the wood. It does not therefore, specifically depend upon penetrating the wood in order to adhere and can generally be safely used on highly resinous woods. It is applied with a fairly stiff brush, the initial strokes in the direction of the grain to force the primer into close contact with the wood. The surface is then diagonally brushed over, to smooth out any paint ridges and finally is brushed lightly up and down the grain. The work is then laid aside to dry, after which it is lightly sanded to remove any "nibs" or small clots of paint as they are termed.

Undercoat

This should be a "flat" coat, i.e. one without a glossy finish. Undercoats are usually grey or pink in colour, depending upon the colour of the final coat. If this is to be white or cream, a pink undercoat is best, as a grey one may show through the top coat. It is applied evenly and is well brushed out and is left to dry thoroughly.

Top Coat

This will be the glossy coat and as such has a greater capacity to flow level than the undercoat. At the same time it must be applied as evenly as possible and the brush should be worked towards the edges. Start the strokes *on* the surface of the wood so that the brush always *leaves* an edge. This avoids piling up the paint on the corners which may harden into globules or as a ridge, which is termed a "fat-edge".

Drying

A word or two must be said about drying. Oil Paints dry mainly by oxidation and not by evaporation as is often supposed. It is therefore important that sufficient time is allowed for each coat to thoroughly "dry out" before the next is applied. You may find that after an hour or two, the surface appears dry to the touch but this, in fact, is only the skin of the paint. Underneath there is probably a semi fluid layer which has not yet had time to dry thoroughly and which unless allowed to do so may cause cracking or peeling if another coat is put on. It is always safest, therefore, to allow about twenty-four hours for each coat to dry, if the finish is to be good and lasting.

Two Colour Work

It is of course obvious that when using two finishing colours on a toy they should be separately applied, the second colour only when the first has properly dried. Another important point to watch is that the two paints are similar in chemical composition. If this simple precaution is not observed you may find that at the junction of the two paints they will react one with the other to produce a horrid "bubbly" mess! So long as the same "family" of paint or enamel is used there should be no difficulty in obtaining a clean junction line but in case of doubt it is a simple operation to try out the two on a piece of scrap wood.

So much for a plain junction between two colours, but what about dividing lines or bands? These may be put down between two similar or dissimilar colours and the criterion is obviously a line of uniform width if the work is to be successful.

At first sight it seems a simple job to paint a line say 1/8 in. wide on a flat surface but experiment will prove just how difficult it can be unless the job is tackled the right way. The method is to lay down two chalk guide lines spaced apart exactly to the width of the band. These are produced by running a length of cotton over a stick of chalk, stretching the cotton over the surface in the exact position of one edge of the band, then plucking the cotton vertically. Repeat to give the limit for the other edge of the band. It is now a simple job to paint between the chalk lines and as a further aid to straight brushing, a ruler can be laid down, overlapping a strip of waste placed on the work. Artists lining brushes are the tools for this job.

Cellulose Lacquer

A superlative finish can be produced with the use of cellulose lacquer but it must be realised at the outset that the work is fairly laborious. At the same time the job is easy to do and does not require specialised equipment. For a large toy such as a doll's pram, the cellulose finish is really worth while and will well repay the extra effort involved.

Cellulose lacquer is applied over specially prepared undercoats which do not react with the cellulose. The ordinary undercoat used for oil paint is not suitable and usually causes the cellulose to "craze" or go into bubbles. The wood is primed in the usual way and whilst primers specially made for cellulose finishing are made, the ordinary type can be used provided that the special undercoat is applied before cellulosing.

The chief difficulty in applying cellulose lacquer arises from its poor qualities of flowing level. As the liquid leaves the brush, it remains in ridges, whereas a high gloss enamel flows to a level surface so that the brush marks "fade out". In the case of cellulose lacquer this disadvantage is accentuated by its extremely rapid drying qualities — it dries in a few minutes — and this makes it even more difficult to produce a flat cellulose surface.

For this reason, cellulose lacquer is usually

applied by the spray method which overcomes the difficulty inherent in the brush technique. By this means the cellulose is applied in an even film, thus the problem of brush marks is overcome. At the same time the film of cellulose will need further levelling which is done in the same way as for the brush technique.

To do so the ridges or inequalities are cut down with emery paper until a smooth level surface is reached. The emery paper used for this process is a waterproof type known as waterproof carborundum paper and is made in various grades. Suitable textures are No. 100 or 120 grade for "first coat" flatting and No. 220 and 320 for succeeding coats. The paper is dipped in water which acts as a lubricant and prevents it being clogged with particles of cellulose and thus producing heavy scratches. Work across the line of ridges, changing to a circular movement until the surface is reasonably flattened. This process may well cut right through the cellulose film in the early stages and expose the undercoat. The surface is then swabbed, wiped off with a clean rag and allowed to dry.

Several coats are applied in this way until the cellulose surface is built up level, when the final gloss can be put on.

Cellulose lacquer dries with a semi-gloss or eggshell finish, the high polish being imparted to it by further processing and is not inherent in the medium. To do this the cellulose is first polished with a fine grade "metal" polish such as chromium plate polish. No special procedure is necessary except that the finishing strokes of the polishing pad should be in one direction only. The surface is then wiped over and treated with wax polish to produce the final high gloss.

Staining and Polishing

This is a suitable method of finishing a number of wood toys. Spirit stains should always be used as the water soluble variety can usually be licked off! These stains are sometimes obtainable in liquid form but more usually they are sold as a powder. Dissolved in methylated spirit according to the quantity stated on the packet, they produce full rich colours with little effort. They dry rapidly and for this reason are more difficult to apply evenly to large surfaces than are water stains. It is always advisable to apply a coat of polish or varnish after staining in order to fix the stain to make sure it will not come off.

French polish applied over the spirit stains will produce a good finish and for the lighter colours white french polish should be used. If it is unobtainable locally, it can be made by dissolving 6 ozs. of bleached shellac in one pint of methylated spirits.

For a varnished finish, white hard spirit varnish is the best to use. It dries quickly but is a little more trouble to apply than oil varnish. Its advantage, however, lies in the fact that it does not become tacky if the toy is allowed to stand before a fire.

Producing a smooth evenly varnished surface is sometimes rather a problem as the stickly surface "picks up" any dust or fluff which may be floating about. This settles on the surface and becomes embedded, to be covered by the next coat of varnish unless something is done about it.

Firstly, the best solution is to avoid dust, which however obvious it seems is quite a problem in itself. Moderately damping down the floor is a good plan but must not be overdone or the humidity of the workshop may easily be raised to an extent which will cause "bloom" to appear in the varnished work.

Open windows are also to be avoided for

obvious reasons and the bench should be dusted down some little time before varnishing commences.

Pimples which have appeared in spite of these precautions can best be eased down with a scrap of worn No. "o" glasspaper which has been moistened and dabbed with soap. The latter acts as a lubricant and prevents undue scratching of the surface. The parts will of course subsequently need to be re-varnished.

"Wallart"

Manufactured by Winsor and Newton Limited, "Wallart" is a plastic modelling medium which can be used on toys to produce most realistic "concrete" and other surfaces. It consists of a white powder which, mixed with water to a smooth paste, is brushed on to the surfaces to be treated. It adheres to almost any type of surface and can be stippled or textured in many different ways limited only by the worker's own ingenuity. This surface treatment is, of course, done whilst the "Wallart" is still wet.

Upon drying, the medium can be painted or enamelled to any desired colour and is frequently used to produce relief maps of geographical features. It may also be carved after drying and this, in conjunction with texturing or stippling, may be used to achieve many distinctive effects. Full information about "Wallart" may be obtained in a descriptive leaflet obtainable from Winsor and Newton Ltd., Wealdstone, Harrow, Middlesex, or from handicraft stores stocking the material.

Chapter IV

NURSERY TOYS

DESIGNED to be instructive as well as to give amusement to the youngster, nursery toys form a significant part of the child's early training. Shapes, colours and simple mechanisms all combine to help the child to appreciate the functions of the objects around it.

Dowel Box

Shown in Fig. 3, this is a simple box with a base which swings open to allow the dowels to be removed. The top is composed of two pieces of thin ply with a strip of rubber cut from an old cycle inner tube sandwiched between them. The openings in the ply pieces are cut with a fretsaw whilst the two parts are clamped together. This ensures that they are exactly alike. The rubber is then clamped between the two parts and the openings marked with a soft pencil. Similar openings are cut in the rubber with a razor blade or really sharp knife and are made slightly smaller than those in the ply. The rubber/ply sandwich is then glued and clamped together until dry. An excellent glue for this purpose is Rawlplug "Durofix", manufactured by the Rawlplug Company Ltd. The completed top is screwed to the sides and the pivot block for the base is fixed in place. The base and end stops are then fixed in position. The shaped dowels are cut from hardwood and have bevelled ends to allow them to spread the rubber as they are knocked through the openings in the top. When they are nearly through the openings, the bevels also allow them to spring forward on the last mallet blow and they drop into the box with a satisfying plonk! The dowels themselves must, of course, not be too tight a fit in the shaped openings and they should be really well smoothed so that there will be no chance of the child encountering splinters.

The mallet is made from a length of 1/4 in. dowel rod glued into a short piece of broomstick or other round material. Again emphasis is on smoothing and the dead square ends of the head are best taken off with glasspaper.

The box is finished by enamelling in a bright

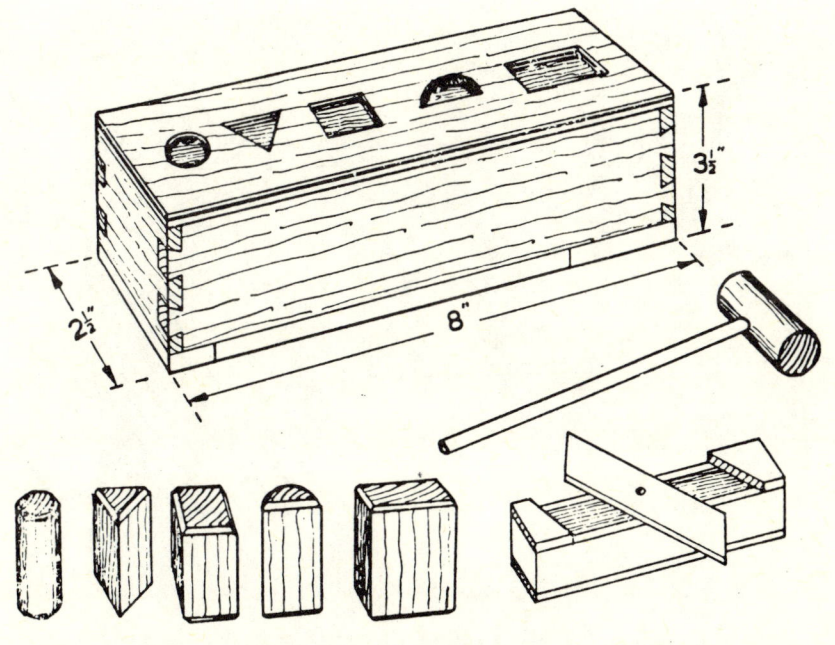

Fig. 3.   Dowel Box

Fig. 4. Double Jig-Saw Puzzle

colour, whilst the dowels are either left plain or may themselves be coloured. This is done with spirit stain which is afterwards fixed with a coat of french polish, to make quite sure that the child will come to no harm by trying to lick off the colours!

Double Jig Saw Picture

Suitable for young children, this toy shown in Fig. 4 also provides instruction in recognising shapes and the association of colours. The construction is apparent, the "book" consisting of a double sandwich of plywood which is hinged with scraps of leather and kept closed with an elastic band. There are thus no sharp projections on which the child might catch its clothes or fingers.

Any suitable picture is selected, bearing in mind that the criterion is one with bold subjects and absence of very small detail. The selected picture, or preferable a carbon copy, is pasted on to a piece of thin plywood, which is then clamped to the second piece of ply. These parts are fretted together so that the cut-outs will be interchangeable. Prepare the two backing plys and cut the recesses for the leather hinges and pins (these are cut from wire paper fasteners), also the recesses for the elastic and its pins. The hinges and elastic are then glued in place as shown in the inset sketch, following which the "background" leaves are also glued on. Small holes are then drilled through the backing plies to enable a matchstick to be used to push out the fret parts if they become jammed in place.

Colouring the parts must, of course, be left to the reader's own devices. The object is to produce brightly coloured pictures but to arrange the colours in such a way that the fret parts may be interchanged between the leaves to give a variety of pictures. The need for a bold, simple basic design will be apparent. Oil colours are the best to use, a recommended brand being Winsor and Newton's Artists Oil Colours. These are manufactured from high-grade materials and are a perfectly safe medium for this type of toy. They can be obtained in 2 in. tubes, thus making it economical to buy a number of colours for even a single toy. The backing leaves can be coloured in the same mediums or with Winsor & Newton's Decorative Art Oil Colours, obtainable in "Q4" Tubes which contain approximately four fluid ounces of colour. These colours are of the same quality and permanence as the Artists Oil Colours but are not ground quite so finely. They are specially produced for high class decorative work apart from oil painting.

Toy Bricks

Always a popular toy with young children, the toy bricks shown in Fig. 5 provide an endless source of enjoyment. The box is made with 1/2 in. thick hardwood sides, front and back whilst the sliding lid and base are 1/4 in. plywood or hardboard. Commence by cutting a piece of hardwood 22.1/4 in. long by 2.1/8 in. wide. This will be used for the sides and back and is separated after the groove for the sliding lid has been worked. The groove itself is 1/4 in. wide by 1/4 in. deep and is spaced 1/4 in. from the edge as shown in the detail sketch Fig. 5. The three parts are cut to length and the front, which is 1/2 in. narrower than the other parts, is also cut at this stage.

The box frame is through dovetailed and glued together, care being taken to see that it is square and is not in winding. The ends of the groove in the back member will of course show and this cannot be avoided without using a more complicated form of corner joint. With care, however, the square holes can be filled with plastic wood but be sure that the grooves are clear at the corners.

The base is now cut from 1/4 in. ply or hardboard and is best screwed in place. A slight overlap is allowed all round which is trimmed back flush when the fixing is complete. The top is next cut and trimmed to size and a 1/2 in. by 1/4 in. fillet is glued along the top front edge as shown.

The blocks are cut from 1.1/2 in. square hardwood (beech if possible) and the best method is to smooth and glasspaper the lengths prior to cutting. Careful measuring and sawing is required and the dead square corners are taken off with a chisel followed by glasspapering. The end grain should be thoroughly smoothed with grades 1 and "o" glasspaper, after which the blocks are given a coat of glue size to seal the grain. They are then rubbed down smooth with No. "o" glasspaper and given a coat of primer or undercoating. This in turn is rubbed down with No. "o" glasspaper and the top enamel coats are put on. A good decoration scheme to use is three colours, each block having opposite faces of the same colour. This allows all the blocks to be packed together and one face of each block enamelled in

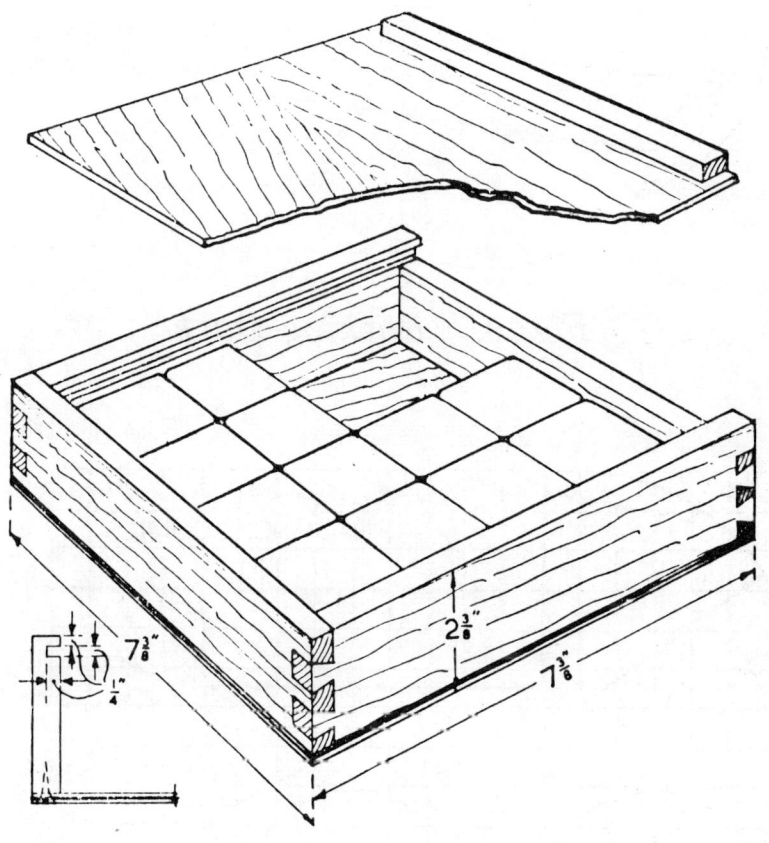

Fig. 5. **Toy Bricks**

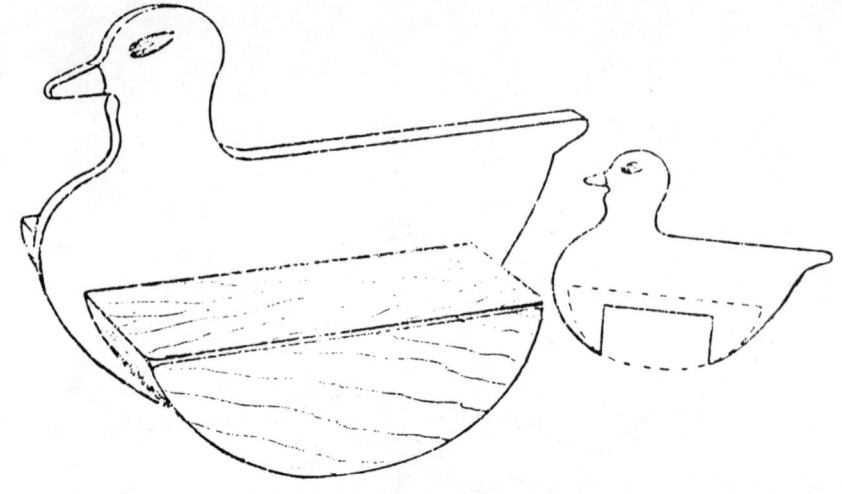

Fig. 6.   Rocking Duck

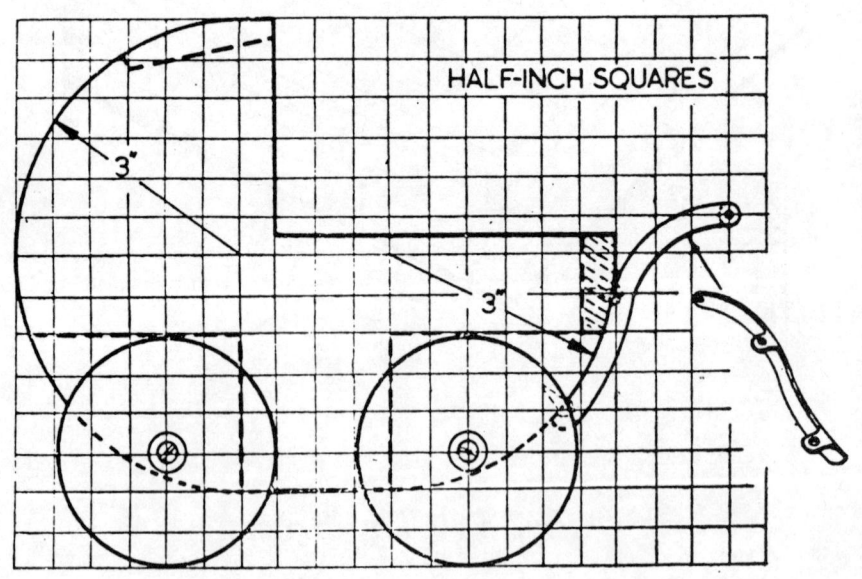

HALF-INCH SQUARES

3"

3"

Fig. 7.   Miniature Doll's Pram

a single operation. When dry, reverse the pack and enamel all the "reverse" faces. The remainder of the colouring is done on similar lines. If desired, small decorative transfers can now be applied to some or all of the blocks.

The box is best finished by staining and polishing. Spirit stain should be used and is fixed with two coats of polish which will give a reasonable shine.

Rocking Duck

This toy makes no pretence to instructional value but is, nevertheless, a favourite with young children. Various animal shapes could be used, though the duck seems to be the most popular. Fig. 6 gives the details and it will be seen that the rocker is solid with a housing cut out to receive the animal shape. This is drawn on 3/16 in. or 1/4 in. ply and is glued into the housing. The toy is then enamelled in bright colours. An enlargement on the scheme is to make two or three small "ducklings" scaled down from the original toy and enamelled in the same colours.

Miniature Doll's Pram

A tiny doll's pram is a fascinating toy for

young children and can be made most attractive if enamelled in bright colours. Fig. 7 shows the details and the whole toy, except for the wheels, can be made from scraps. The sides are cut from 1/16 in. ply, the best way being to clamp two pieces together and saw both parts in one operation.

The pram is 3.1/2 in. wide but of course this is not shown in the side elevation Fig. 7. The two wooden blocks which form the seats are trimmed to profile before they are pinned into place with 1 in. oval nails. Final trimming is done with a block plane which is followed by glasspapering smooth. Another shaped block is used at the rear end of the pram and measures 1.1/4 in. wide by 1/2 in. thick before being tapered and worked to profile. It is fixed in place with 1 in. oval nails, final trimming to profile being done afterwards.

To stiffen the hood a block measuring 2 in. wide by 1/4 in. thick is shaped to profile and pinned between the sides. This can be cut from a scrap of hardwood. A flat block 2 in. wide by 1/4 in. thick is pinned at the base of the pram, between the seat blocks. This enables the curved ply to be fixed at its central point and prevents it bowing away.

The curved part of the toy is cut from 1/16 in. thick ply, the strip being 3.5/8 in. wide by about 18 in. long. This will allow for an overlap at the sides and ends which is trimmed away after fixing. The strip is cut with the grain of the outer plies running across it and will then easily bend to the curves required. To fix it in place, coat about 3 in. of one face with glue, brush glue on the hood stiffening block and fix the end of the strip in place with 1/4 in. veneer pins. Coat a little more of the strip with glue and brush glue on the first seat block. Bend round the strip and fix down with veneer pins. Work in this way until the profile is covered, then lay aside to dry. The overlaps are then trimmed away and the whole toy glasspapered smooth ready for the finishing processes.

The handle parts are cut from thin brass or aluminium sheet, the profile being shown in Fig. 7. The two lugs are bent at right angles and drilled for the small round-head wood screws used for fixing to the carcase. The handle proper is a length of 1/4 in. dowel rod fixed by small round head or raised head screws.

The carcase, handle parts and wheels are enamelled separately and afterwards fixed in place. Bright colours are best for this toy, a contrast being made between the interior and exterior surfaces. It is also a good plan to have the wheels a different colour to the pram body, the best effect being to make these match the interior colour. Chromium plated round head screws are used as pivots and spacing washers should be employed to prevent the wheels rubbing against the pram sides.

Earth Dumper

This is a familiar machine seen where road construction or airfield work is in progress. The appeal of this toy to young children lies mainly in the tipping action of the hod which is tilted by depressing the lever which projects at the side. Small objects may be loaded into the hod and the toy trundled round to tip its load at the whim of its young "driver".

Fig. 8 shows the details and the construction is not at all complicated. The main platform is 3/8 in. thick and the axle blocks are cut from hardwood and screwed in place. Notice that one is deeper than the other to allow for the difference in the wheel sizes and the consequently different heights of the axles. A pair of 2 in. wheels are used at the front with 1 in. wheels behind.

The front part of the main platform is thickened with 1/4 in. ply glued and screwed in place and recessed for a small hinge. Notice that the hinge is let wholly into the thicknessing piece so that the base of the hod lies down flush. Advantage may then be taken of the full 3/8 in. thickness of the hod-base to afford a good purchase for the hinge screws.

Behind the thickness piece on the main platform is another piece of 1/4 in. ply having a rounded front edge. It is fixed with tiny hinges and carries a handle cut from brass sheet to enable it to be raised to the upright position. By doing this, the back of the hod is raised and the contents tipped out.

The engine casing is a block of softwood glued in place and carries the seat which is cut from scraps and glued on. The steering wheel is a wood or fibre disc mounted on a length of 3/16 in. dowel rod glued into a hole bored in the main platform. The hod sides are cut from 3/16 in. ply and are through dovetailed together. Casein glue is used for strength purposes when glueing the parts together. The base of the hod is cut from 3/8 in. hardwood and carefully trimmed to size. An adjustable bevel is used to check that the angle of the sides corresponds with the hod. Fix in place with casein glue and reinforce with panel pins driven through the sides.

Bright yellow enamel is used for finishing this toy.

Goods Train

This toy is always a great favourite with little boys, particularly if a variety of wagons are made. The engine is shown in Fig. 9 and is of simple yet robust construction.

The boiler is a 4 in. length of 2 in. diameter wooden rod and has two 1/2 in. diameter recesses bored in it for the smoke stack and steam dome, each cut from dowel rod and glued in place. Two shaped cradles support the boiler, they are glued to the base and the boiler itself is fixed by screwing up through the base and these cradles.

The cab and tender are combined, and are cut from 1/4 in. thick hardwood or plywood. The cab front is pierced with two window openings each formed by boring three 1/4 in. holes as shown in the front elevation. The final shaping is done with a small chisel and is finished by glasspapering smooth. Pin the cab front to the

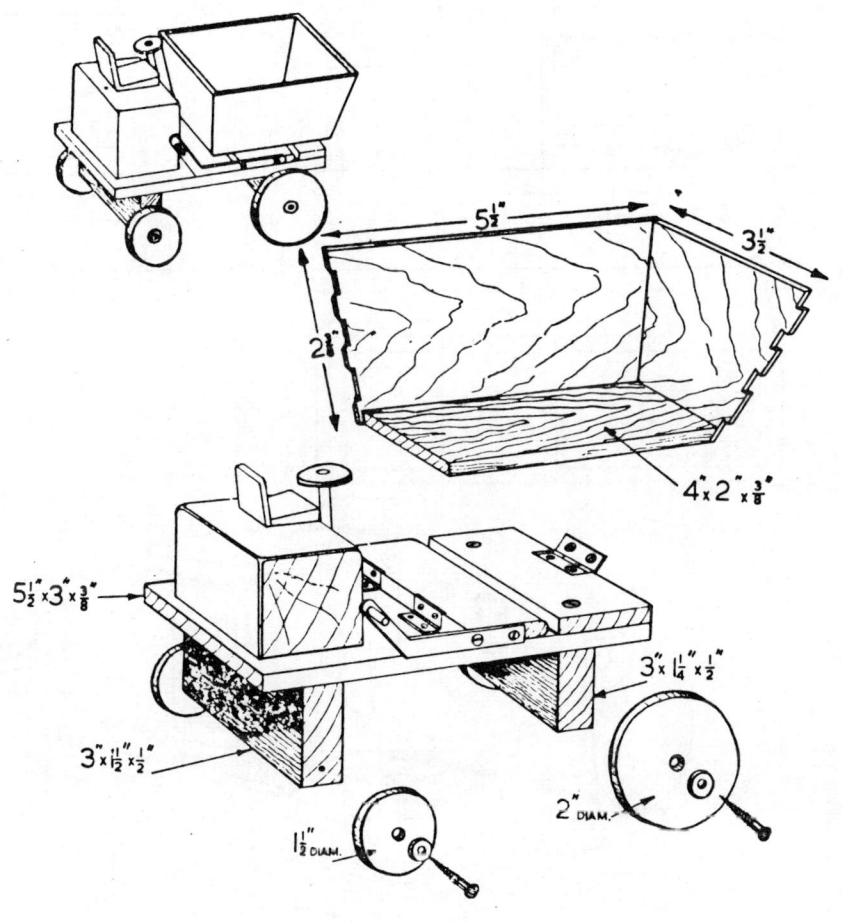

Fig. 8.   Earth Dumper

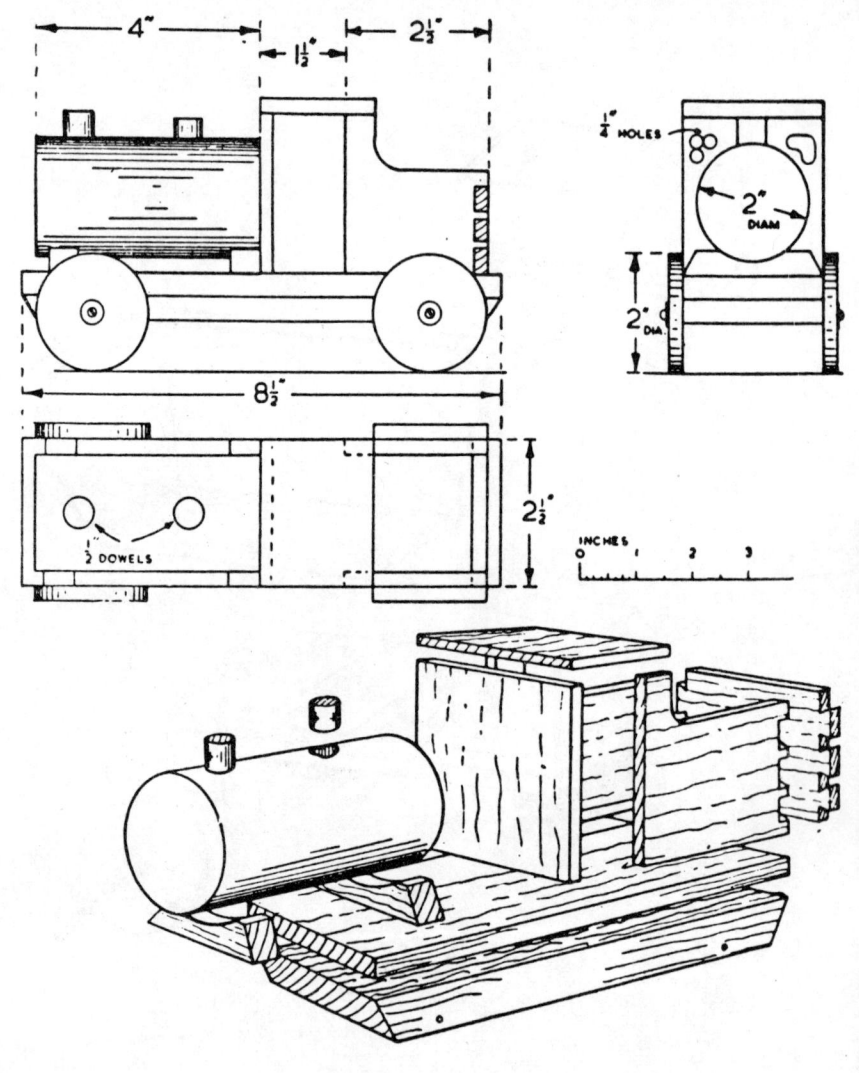

Fig. 9.   Toy Engine

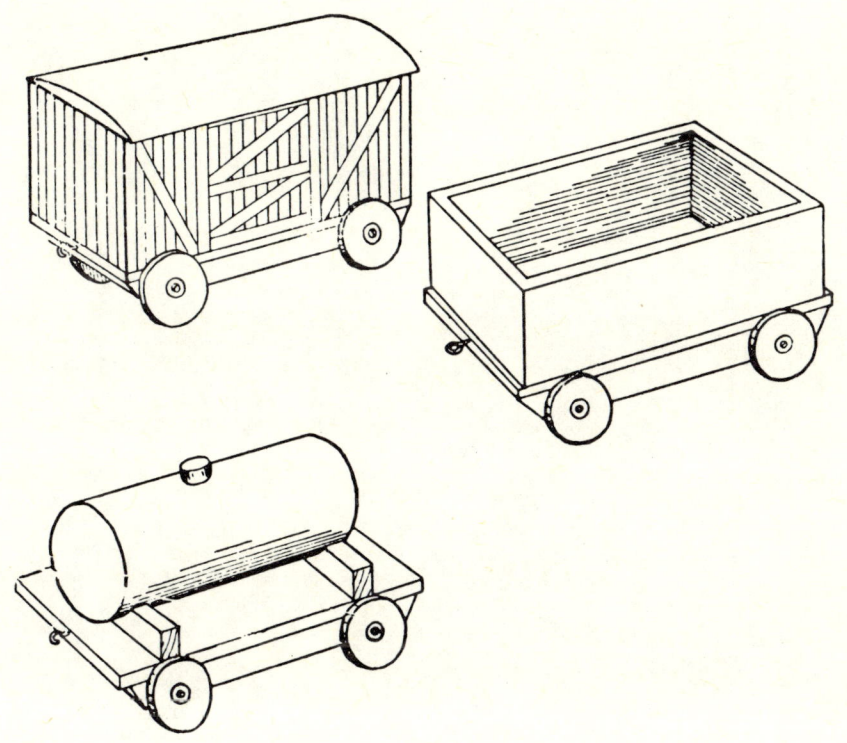

Fig. 10.   Rolling Stock

rear end of the boiler and by screwing up through the base. The sides and back of the tender are dovetailed together as shown and are fixed by pinning up through the base. The cab roof is also in 1/4 in. ply and is pinned on.

A shaped wooden block to carry the wheels is screwed under the base. The wheels are 2 in. diameter and are pivoted on screws and fitted with washers. A small cup hook is fixed at the rear of the base and turned so that it is open side face downwards. This minimises the chance of the child catching its hand on the end of the hook if it falls on the toy. A screw-eye is used at the front for towing.

Fig. 10 shows three types of wagon, all of which should be made to the same scale as the loco. The bases and shaped wheel pivot blocks are standardised and are fitted with a hook at one end and an eye at the other. The sides of the closed wagon are 1/4 in. ply dovetailed together and fixed by screwing up through the base. The roof is a shaped block rebated all round the underside so that it fits easily between the walls. It is left loose so that it may be lifted off for the wagon to be loaded with small objects. The planking is done by scoring with a sharp knife and steel rule, before the wagon is painted. Two cuts are made for each line to produce a narrow V-shaped groove. The wagon is then painted, after which the planking lines can be blacked in with a fine paint brush.

The open truck needs little explanation and is made on similar lines to the closed wagon. The sides are, of course, not so high and are dovetailed together from 1/4 in. ply. The toy can either be left plainly painted or can be scored and planked in the same manner as the closed wagon.

Construction of the tank wagon is also on simple lines. The tank is made from the same diameter material as the loco boiler and is mounted in the same way. One or more filling ports may be used and the tank could be labelled "Petrol" or "Milk", etc.

Chapter V

TOYS FOR BOYS

THE first four toys in this chapter are designed as accessories to the model railway. The most usual size is gauge "O" for which these accessories have been scaled, and on which all the measurements given have been based. There is, of course, no reason why the toys should not be made smaller for, say gauge "OO" track, but this is left to the readers own requirements.

Tunnel

This is perhaps the first accessory which the average young railway enthusiast demands and is therefore certain to be eagerly welcomed. The details are shown in Fig. 11 and the tunnel has been made large enough to span double gauge "O" tracks. These are permanently fixed to the baseboard of the toy and ensure that the rolling stock will not collide in the tunnel.

The baseboard itself is a piece of 1/4 in. thick

hardboard measuring 14 in. long by 16 in. wide. The four main pillars are 3/4 in. square and are grooved 1/4 in. × 1/4 in. on their "inside" faces for the tunnel end pieces. A 1/4 in. × 1/4 in. stopped groove is worked on the "outer" face of each pillar to hold the tunnel restraining walls, which, like the end pieces are cut from 1/4 in. thick hardboard. The restraining wall pillars are 3/4 in. square and are grooved on the inside faces for the ends of the restraining walls. All the pillars are secured by screwing up through the baseboard.

The tunnel proper is made of cardboard bent to a 3 in. radius, the vertical sides being 2.1/4 in. high. It is glued between side boards measuring 12.1/2 in. × 3.1/2 in. × 1/2 in. and fixed by screwing up through the baseboard. A 1 in. × 3/4 in. batten fixed between the tunnel end pieces immediately over the tunnel roof, reinforces the structure.

The contour of the tunnel is built up in papier-mâché laid over hardboard and cardboard supports. Two sheets of hardboard are pinned to triangular fillets glued to the baseboard and tunnel side boards as indicated in Fig. 11. A sheet of cardboard is pinned over the tunnel and

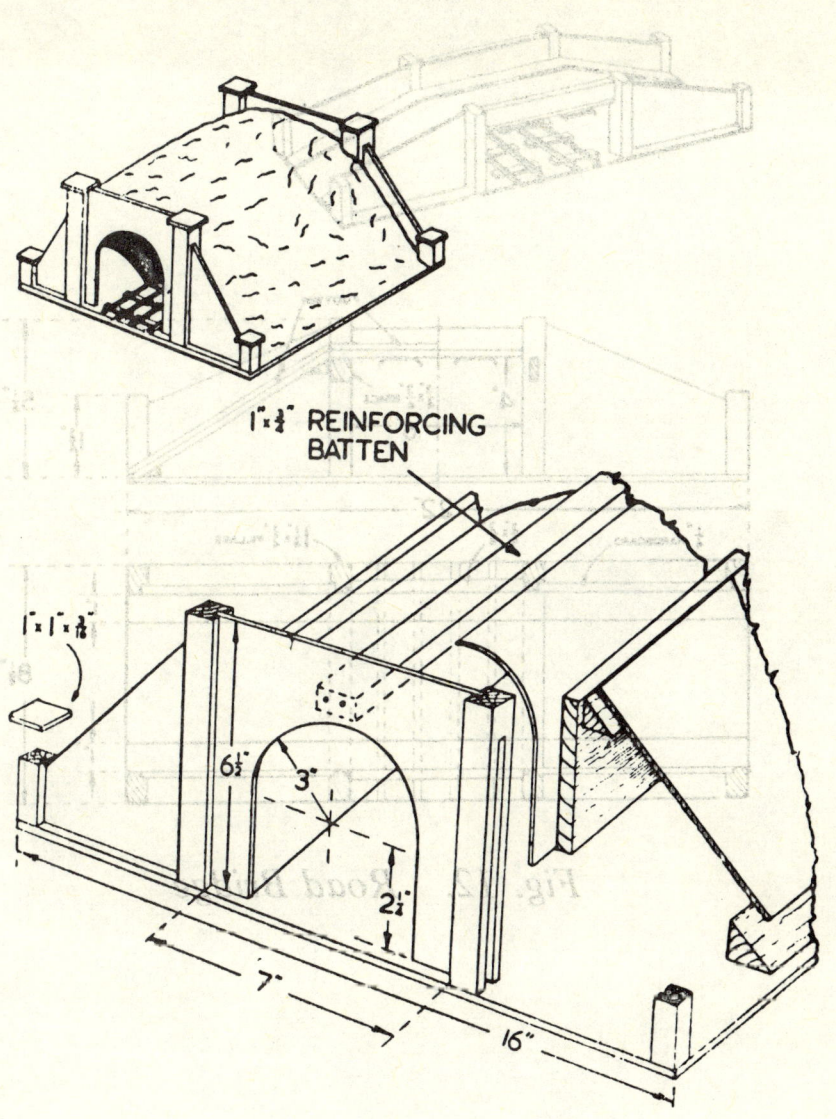

1"×⅜" REINFORCING BATTEN

1"×1"×⅞"

6½"

3"

2¼"

7"

16"

Fig. 11.   Railway Tunnel

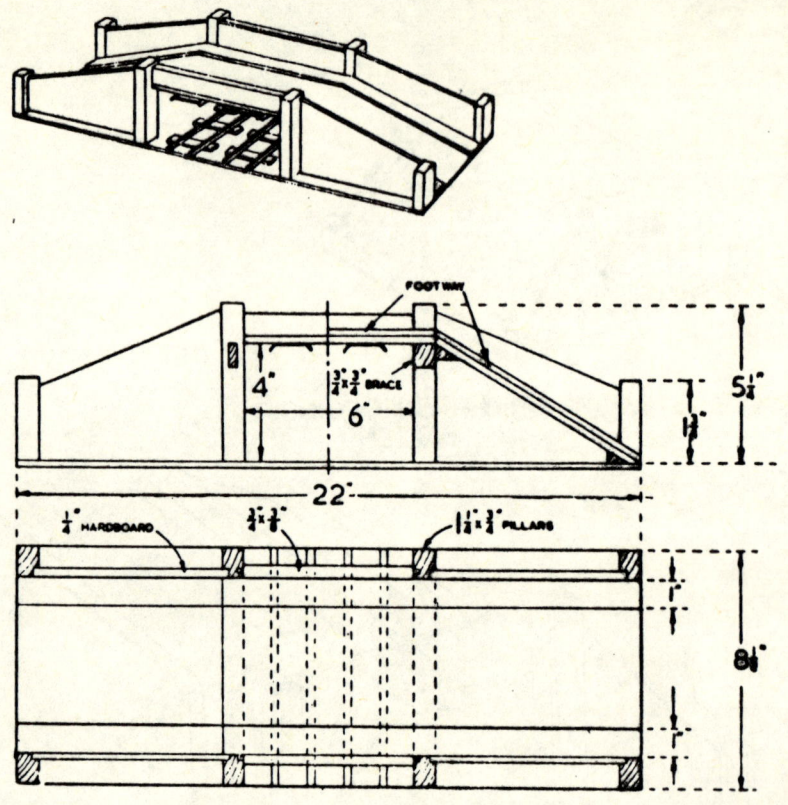

Fig. 12.   Road Bridge

is fixed to the side boards and the top batten. The papier-mâché is then laid on and secured here and there with veneer pins. When really dry it is coloured in shades of green and brown. The tunnel ends and restraining walls may be treated with Winsor and Newton's "Wallart" textured to represent concrete, or as an alternative they may be covered with dolls-house "brick" paper.

Road Bridge

Shown in Fig. 12, this toy also has been designed to span two tracks of gauge "O" metals but could easily be re-scaled for "single line" working. The base of the toy is cut from 1/4 in. thick hardboard, which is also used for the approach walls. The road and footway pieces are 3/16 in. thick hardboard.

All the pillars are cut from 1.1/4 in. × 3/4 in. hardwood and are fixed by screwing up through the base. The main pillars are arranged in two pairs, each having a 3/4 in. square bearer tenoned between them. The central road piece is pinned to these bearers under the bridge sides and fixed by screwing up underneath. The bridge sides are 3/4 in. × 3/8 in. hardwood stub-tenoned into the main pillars.

The approach walls are glued into rebates worked in the pillars. These rebates can best be worked whilst the material is still "in the length" that is, before it is cut to size. The open ends of the rebates left after the walls are glued in place can be filled with plastic wood as the toy will be painted or otherwise finished.

To support the approach roadway pieces, four triangular section strips are glued in place as shown in Fig. 12. The road pieces are pinned in place and the footway strips are fixed with glue. In order to give realism to the toy, a pair of smoke shields are cut from cardboard and glued under the bridge. The cardboard is cut out and scored on the upper face for bending. This is done over a chamfered wood strip and the top surface is then covered with paper which is gummed in place. This reinforces the bends and holds the shields up to shape.

An excellent finish for this toy is Winsor and Newton's "Wallart" already mentioned earlier in this book. It is brushed on and textured to represent concrete. Ordinary flat paint is a good medium for the road and footway surfaces.

Railway Station

This toy is shown at Fig. 13, together with the working drawings. The base could be made wide enough to carry a length of gauge "O" track as shown in the perspective sketch, the track being permanently screwed in place.

Plywood or hardboard is used almost exclusively in this toy. The base is 3/16 in. thick whilst the platform walls and surfaces are 1/4 in. thick. The platform walls are pinned to two wooden blocks measuring 3.1/2 in. $\times$ 1.1/2 in. $\times$ 1 in. They are chamfered to receive the platform ramps and are glued to the base. A couple of 1 in. countersunk screws driven up through the base into each block, reinforces the joints.

The platform top is 11 ins. long and is trimmed square at the ends. It is pinned to the support blocks and the heads of the pins are punched down and filled over with plastic wood or stopping. The platform ramps are bevelled to fit neatly in position against the top and also against the base. These are secured with glue and pins driven into the support blocks.

The walls of the waiting room are cut from 3/16 in. hardboard, the corners being mitred together. Openings for the windows and door are cut out with a fretsaw. The window openings are "glazed" with pieces of thin cellulose acetate or "Perspex" and to represent the window bars, these are scored with a sharp point such as a bradawl and the channels thus made are filled in with black or white paint. The material is cut slightly larger than the window openings and is fixed in place with Rawlplug "Durofix".

Pieces of moulding or strips of model aircraft spar material are glued to the platform top to act as support fillets for the waiting room walls. These are glued in place and the joints reinforced with one or two veneer pins on each wall. More fillets are used around the top inside edges of the walls and these also provide fixings for the roof, which is cut from 3/16 in. hardboard. The roof pelmets are strips of model aircraft material cut with a sharp knife to form the drip-points. The completed strips are fixed in position with glue and the whole roof is pinned in place.

Strip material as used for model aircraft construction is employed to make the station fences, the scheme being shown in Fig. 13. The palings are cut from 1/4 in. × 1/8 in. material and are pointed at one end and glued to the top rail (of 1/4 in. × 1/8 in. strip). Two lengths of

1/8 in. × 1/8 in. strip are glued along the back edge of the platform and the fences are stood against them. Two more lengths of 1/8 in. × 1/8 in. stuff are glued against the bottoms of the palings and the surface of the platform. The end posts are 1/4 in. square rounded at the lower ends and glued into holes bored in the platform top. The top rails are bevelled at the ends and glued into V-shaped notches cut in the end posts with a sharp knife. Balsa cement is the best type of adhesive to use in the construction of the fences, although at the same time, a little Winsor and Newton's "Wallart" mixed to a paste with water and pressed into the channel between the palings will hold them rigidly in place.

An alternative to the open fences would be "walls" of thin material glued between quarter-round mouldings also glued to the platform top. The ends could be supported in grooves cut in the length of the end posts.

Suitable decorative finish for this toy would be "Wallart" for the platform walls and waiting room, and paint on the remainder of the surfaces. Colour schemes would be to individual choice, though the youngster may object if anything but the authentic British Rail scheme is used!

Turntable

Shown in Fig. 14, this toy is quite easily made and will afford the youngster endless amusement. The base is cut from 3/16 in. hardboard, care being taken to see that the pivot holes for the turntable and winding gear spindle are accurately located.

The turntable ring is cut from 1 in. thick hardboard, the inside diameter is 7 in. whilst the outer diameter is 11 in. A 1/2 in. diameter hole is bored through the width of the rim to allow the winding gear cord to pass through. The angle at which this hole is bored is best obtained by laying the ring on a full-scale drawing of the toy on which a line has been drawn and joining the centres of the two pivot holes. The marks are then squared across the thickness of the ring and joined in pencil across the width. This allows the angle of the hole to be "sighted" and the bit can then be kept at the correct angle whilst boring the hole. When completed, the ring is glued to the 3/16 in. hardboard base and the ramp is made and glued in place. This is cut from softwood, the convex end being shaped with a bowsaw.

The turntable is a 7 in. diameter disc of 3/16 in.

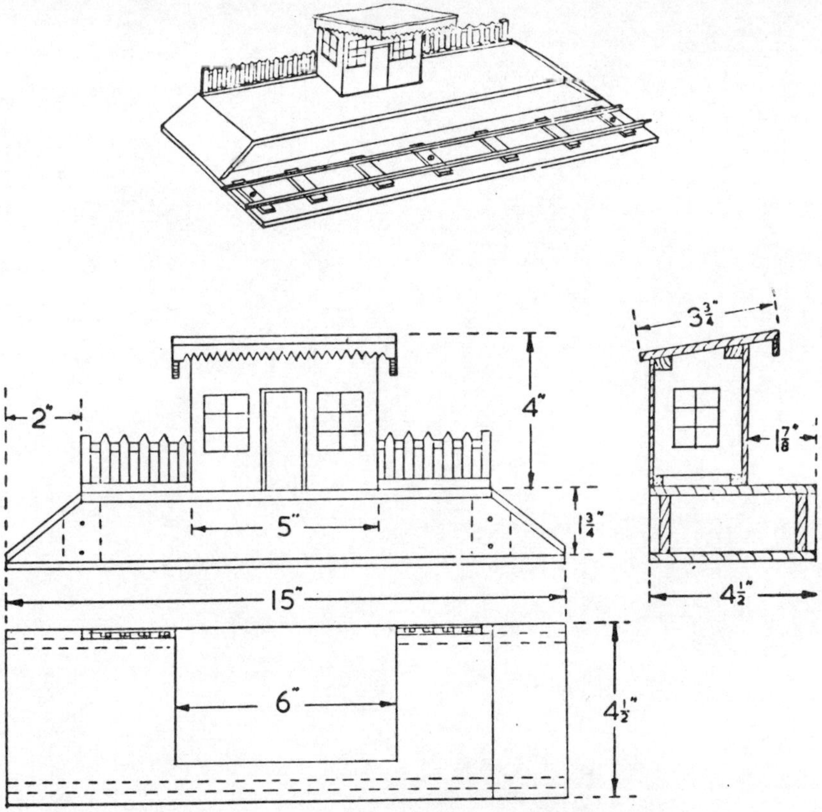

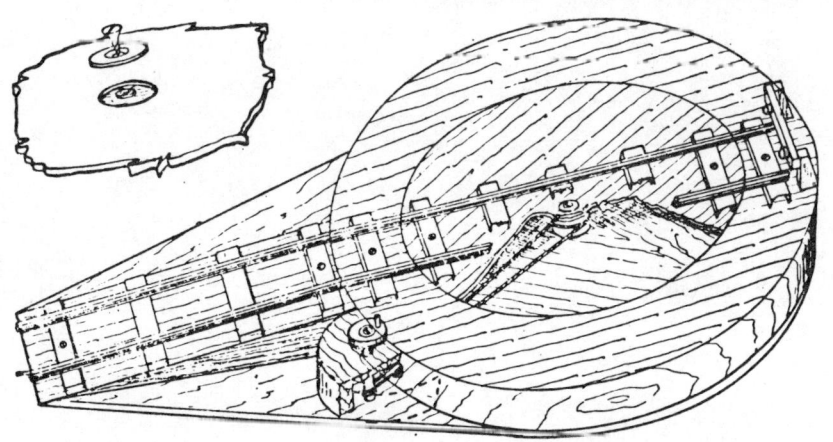

Fig. 13.   Toy Railway Station

Fig. 14.   Railway Turntable

thick hardboard marked out and carefully cut to size with a bowsaw. The final edge smoothing is done with a sharp spokeshave. It rests on a large cotton reel which is cut to length. The central hole is bored out 3/16 in. diameter and a length of 3/16 in. dowel rod glued in place and trimmed flush at the top and projects slightly at the lower end. A V-shaped groove is cut round the reel in which the winding cord rests. The reel is fixed to the turntable with two small countersunk screws. At the lower end the projecting dowel enters a 3/16 in. hole bored in the base and is trimmed to project slightly proud of a shallow recess cut in the underside of the base to contain a washer and countersunk screw. The washer is of course countersunk and the screw is driven into the end of the dowel and thus prevents the turntable being lifted off. To guard against the turntable sagging when the loco is run on, three small wheels taken from curtain rail fittings are fixed inside the turntable-ring, using 1/2 in. round head screws. These support the turntable itself and allow it to revolve freely. One of these "rollers" is placed opposite the end of the ramp, the others at sixty degrees either side.

The winding gear spindle is housed in a shaped

wooden block which is fixed by screwing up through the base. The lower end of the spindle passes through a 1/4 in. hole in the base and is held with a washer and screw in a similar manner to the turntable pivot. The spindle has a V groove cut in it for the winding cord and rotates freely in the hole bored in the block. Two brass washers are used as distance pieces and the top wheel is glued in place. A short length of 1/8 in. dowel rod is glued into this wheel to form a handle.

Although the winding gear may at first present apparent difficulties it is nevertheless a straight-forward job to make. However, a simpler alternative is to omit the puller and cord gear and to fix two square cup hooks into the turntable as handles by which it can be rotated. Be sure to position these so that the screw threads which will of course project through the hardboard, do not foul the three rollers.

All that remains now is to cut lengths of track and screw them in position and to make up the buffers and screw these in place. The uprights for the buffers are glued into notches chiselled in the rim and the joints are reinforced with 1 in. countersunk screws.

Toy Lighthouse

This fascinating toy is shown at Fig. 15 and though at first sight appears to be a complicated project, is actually quite straightforward to make. Electric power for the lantern bulb is supplied by a three-volt twin-cell battery housed in the base and controlled by the "push-on-push-off" switch seen in the illustration. The lantern itself is rotated by turning the wheel projecting from the base and the method by which this is done will be described later.

The base measures 5 in. × 5 in. × 2.1/2. in. The sides are cut from 2 in. × 1/2 in. hardwood and are through dovetailed together at the corners. The top or lid is pinned in place but the base is fixed with countersunk screws in order to be detachable so that the battery can be reached for replacement purposes.

The "No. 800" type "twin cell" battery used has a brass contact on one side, lying between the two cells, whilst another brass contact strip projects from the top of the battery pack. The side contact presses on the head of a round-head screw fixed into the bottom of the spindle and which is electrically connected to the bulb inside the lantern. The other battery contact is connected to the switch. An easy way to do this is to solder a short length of single flex wire to a wire paper clip which is slipped on the battery contact. The other end of the flex is of course connected to one side of the switch. Glue blocks are placed in the base so that the battery can be slipped into position and held there when the bottom is screwed on.

The lighthouse column is made from a length of hardwood measuring 7 in. × 2 in. × 2 in. When finished it is round in section, the base being 2 in. diameter whilst the column tapers to 1.1/2 in. diameter at the top. It is also bored 5/16 in. diameter down the centre to accommodate the spindle and this job may present some difficulty unless tackled carefully.

Fig. 16 shows how the work may be done. A piece of hardwood measuring 2 in. × 2 in. × 1/2 in. is bored with a 5/16 in. diameter hole exactly in the centre. Two battens each 2 in. wide and 1/2 in. thick and about 8 in. long are screwed to the square block to form a kind of stirrup. The column is now carefully marked at each end with the finished diameters. The centre points are marked and very small short "pilot holes" (each about 1/8 in. deep) are drilled.

These enable the point of the woodwork bit to be accurately located.

The stirrup is then slipped over the column and adjusted so that when the bit is passed through the guide hole and down to the column-top, about 1 in. depth of hole can be bored. This ensures that the bit will follow the axis of the column without being able to tilt from side to side. The hole is bored in stages, lowering the stirrup about 1 inch at a time until the maximum depth is reached. The process is repeated from the opposite end and the two holes will meet exactly, inside the column.

Having completed this part of the work, the column is planed to shape. (A V-shaped planing board is a useful accessory for this job.) After a final smoothing with glasspaper the column is fixed by screwing up through the lid. Use countersunk screws and be sure they do not project.

The 3/16 in. thick, 2.1/2 in. diameter plywood disc for the platform is cut to shape and bored with a 5/16 in. hole to allow the spindle to pass through. Six small holes are bored round the edge to accommodate the handrail supports which are made of stout copper wire. The platform disc is then pinned to the lighthouse column.

To provide a smooth bearing surface on which the lantern disc can revolve, a pot-mender is fixed on the platform as shown in Fig. 15. It is bored out 5/16 in. diameter and small holes are drilled, through which the panel pins can pass. The heads of these pins must not project above the surface or the lantern disc will bind on them, so a centre punch is tapped in the holes which has the effect of countersinking them. The job must be done carefully to avoid buckling the metal, which, being thin, cannot be countersunk in the normal way.

The column is now complete and a start can be made on the spindle and its accessories. The spindle itself is a length of 1/4 in. dowel rod and carries the two lamp wires cemented into grooves cut along its length. This is done with a small carving gouge or a Vee tool, the channels being deep enough to contain the covered bell wire which is cemented in place with Rawlplug "Durofix". Allow it to set hard, then lightly glasspaper away any excess cement.

Equipping the spindle with its various parts is started from the lower end and the first of these is the pulley wheel. This measures about 1.1/4 in. diameter and the central hole is bored out 1/4 in. so that is can be glued to the spindle. A V-shaped groove for the driving cord is cut round the edge of the wheel and one of the lamp wires is gently prised out of its groove as shown in Fig. 15. After the spindle is glued into the pulley, the second lamp wire is bared at the end and formed into a loop. A 3/8 in. round head screw and a brass washer are fitted to the end of the spindle to form a contact for the battery connection as already mentioned.

The first lamp wire is also bared at the end and formed into a loop. A pot-mender is then bored out 1/4 in. at the centre, slipped over the spindle and pinned to the pulley. One of the pins passes through the loop of wire so that it makes a reliable electrical contact. The spindle is thus fitted with two electrical contacts which will rotate with it as it is turned.

To make contact with the pot-mender on the pulley, another pot-mender is fixed under the lid of the base. A wire fixed under this pot-mender is connected to one side of the switch, the diagram being shown in Fig. 16.

The spindle can now be slipped up through the

column and the top accessories mounted. The first of these is a 1.1/2 in. diameter plywood disc bored out 1/4 in. diameter in the centre and glued to the end of the spindle. The two lamp wires are bared at their ends and connected to the miniature batten type holder which is screwed to the disc. A three-volt torch bulb is then screwed into the holder.

The lantern measures 1.1/2 in. tall and is bent to shape. It is made of cellulose acetate sheet or 1/16 in. thick "Perspex" and a butt joint is made where the two edges meet. A 1/4 in. wide strip of acetate or "Perspex" is cemented over this joint inside the cylinder and trimmed flush at each end. The wood disc will need to be recessed for this strip to fit into. Four strips of black enamel are painted inside the cylinder and allowed to dry, after which it is fixed to the disc with short veneer pins. (It will be necessary to bore holes in the lantern for these pins to pass through.) The top cap can then be whittled to shape from a large cotton reel. Alternatively it may be built up from a wooden wheel to fit inside the cylinder, and a piece of round wood pared to a point and cut off to form the cone. The cap is merely pushed in place and may be taken off as required

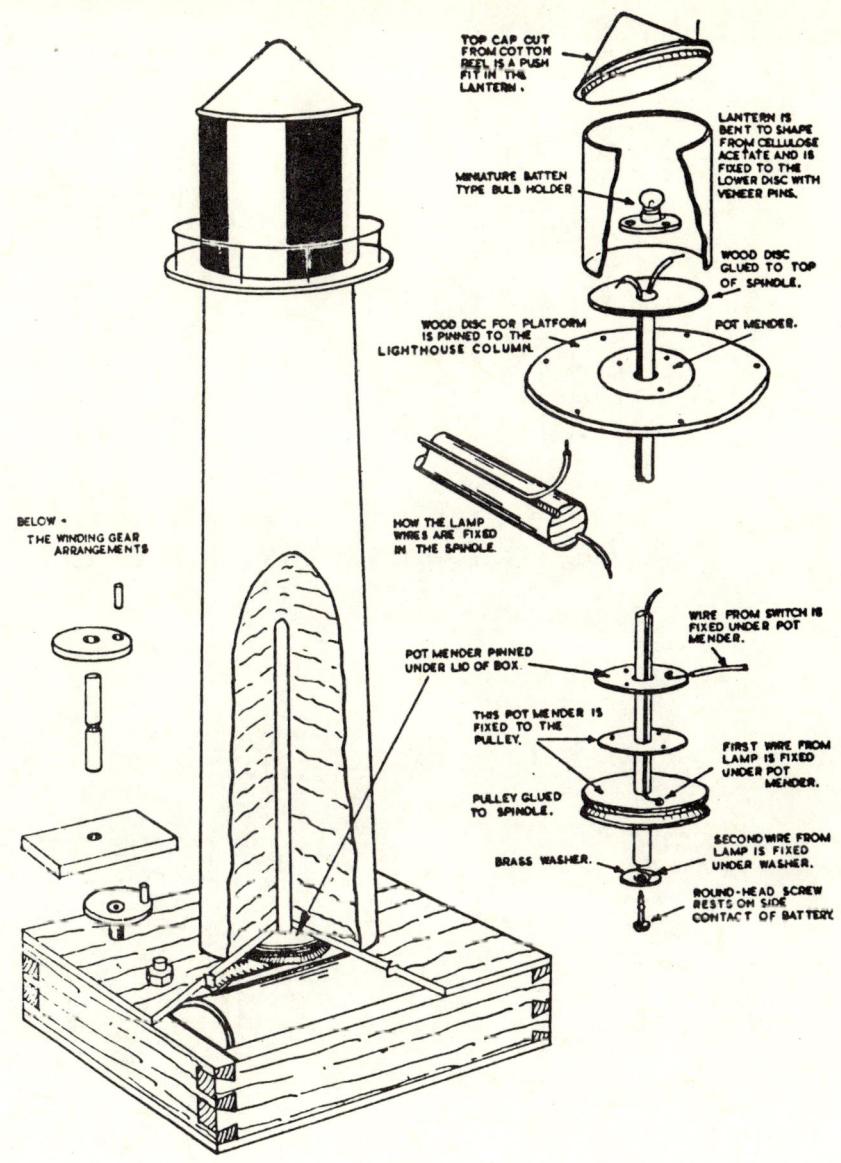

TOP CAP CUT FROM COTTON REEL IS A PUSH FIT IN THE LANTERN.

LANTERN IS BENT TO SHAPE FROM CELLULOSE ACETATE AND IS FIXED TO THE LOWER DISC WITH VENEER PINS.

MINIATURE BATTEN TYPE BULB HOLDER

WOOD DISC GLUED TO TOP OF SPINDLE.

WOOD DISC FOR PLATFORM IS PINNED TO THE LIGHTHOUSE COLUMN.

POT MENDER.

BELOW - THE WINDING GEAR ARRANGEMENTS

HOW THE LAMP WIRES ARE FIXED IN THE SPINDLE.

WIRE FROM SWITCH IS FIXED UNDER POT MENDER.

POT MENDER PINNED UNDER LID OF BOX.

THIS POT MENDER IS FIXED TO THE PULLEY.

FIRST WIRE FROM LAMP IS FIXED UNDER POT MENDER.

PULLEY GLUED TO SPINDLE.

SECOND WIRE FROM LAMP IS FIXED UNDER WASHER.

BRASS WASHER.

ROUND-HEAD SCREW RESTS ON SIDE CONTACT OF BATTERY.

Fig. 15.   Lighthouse

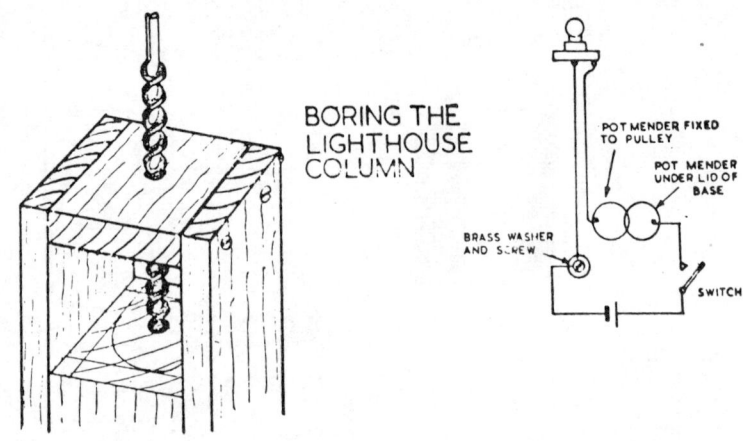

BORING THE
LIGHTHOUSE
COLUMN

POT MENDER FIXED
TO PULLEY

POT MENDER
UNDER LID OF
BASE

BRASS WASHER
AND SCREW

SWITCH

Fig. 16.   Column & Electrical Details

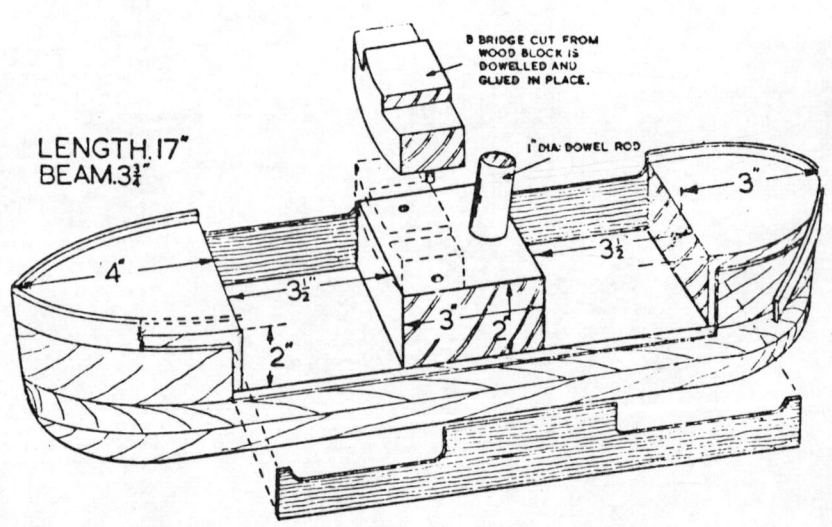

B BRIDGE CUT FROM
WOOD BLOCK IS
DOWELLED AND
GLUED IN PLACE.

LENGTH. 17"
BEAM. 3¾"

1" DIA: DOWEL ROD

3"

4"

3½"

3½"

3"

2"

2"

Fig. 17.   Toy Cargo Ship

should the bulb fail.

The handrail and its supports are next made up and fixed in place. Both are bent from stout copper wire, the uprights being soldered to the rail. The lower ends of the uprights are a push fit in the small holes drilled in the platform and are fixed with a touch of Rawlplug "Durofix".

Arrangement of the winding gear is shown in Fig. 15 and is quite simple. A length of 5/16 in. dowel rod is grooved for the winding cord and passed through a hole in the lid of the base. At its lower end it rests in a hole bored in the small wooden plate which is glued to the bottom of the base. At its upper end it is fitted with a small wood disc and a handle cut from 1/8 in. dowel rod. No provision has been made to prevent it being lifted out as the winding cord will hold it in place. The cord itself is wrapped completely round both the spindle pulley and the winding gear spindle. This ensures a positive drive to the lamp spindle.

This toy can be finished in white enamel throughout or, as an alternative, the base and column may be treated with Winsor and Newton's "Wallart". Another scheme would be to build out the sides of the base with irregularly shaped glue blocks and to coat these with "Wallart" to represent rocks.

Cargo Ship

Shown in Fig. 17, this toy has not primarily been designed to float and no attempt has therefore been made to achieve stability. Upon insistence by the youngster, however, this can be remedied by trial and error by tacking pieces of lead under the hull until the model floats upright. Having thus marked the points which need weighting, recesses are bored in the hull and filled with molten lead. The ends of these lead plugs will be concealed when the toy is painted.

To construct the toy a start is made with the two lowest boards which are each 5/8 in. thick. They are bowsawn roughly to shape and glued together. Casein or synthetic resin glues are used in order to take advantage of their water resistant properties. The completed ship's bottom is trimmed to shape with a spokeshave and a stopped rebate is worked along each edge to receive the sides.

The forecastle, midships and stern blocks are cut from 2 in. thick softwood. The easiest way is to cut the forecastle and stern blocks from one piece of material, separating them after shaping. The material is first bowsawn and the final shaping is done with the spokeshave. Rebates are worked for the ends of the side pieces and the 1/2 in. $\times$ 1/8 in. strips glued round the bows and stern. These are pieces of model aircraft material which are steamed to make them easily pliable and fixed with casein glue and a few veneer pins. Each block in turn is then clamped in position and a couple of 1/4 in. diameter holes are bored up from underneath into the block. When glued to the hull, a pair of 1/4 in. dowels are glued and driven into these holes to reinforce the joints.

The midships block is a length of 3 in. $\times$ 2 in. softwood glued and dowelled in position as before. A 1 in. diameter hole is bored at a slight angle from the vertical to hold the smoke stack which is glued in place. A shaped softwood block is used for the bridge and is glued and dowelled in place as shown in Fig. 17.

The ship is now ready to receive the sides and these are fret sawn to shape from 1/8 in. thick material as used in model aircraft construction. They should be fitted closely in place and fixed with glue and veneer pins. To complete the construction work, holes are bored in the forecastle and stern blocks to receive masts cut from 1/4 in. dowel rod. These are not glued in place as they inevitably get broken sooner or later and are then easily replaced.

The toy is finished in paint or enamel and the first job is to go all over it, filling any crevices, particularly round the side joints, with plastic wood or hard stopping. When dry the surfaces are glasspapered smooth and undercoated. This in turn is glasspapered down and the top coats are put on. It is important that the finish should be allowed to dry thoroughly before the toy is put into water.

Toy Crane

The construction views of this toy are shown in Fig. 18. The bogie platform is cut from 1/4 in. plywood and measures 6 in. × 3.1/2 ins. Two 3/4 in. × 1/2 in. battens are screwed underneath and carry the six 1 in. diameter wooden wheels. These are pivoted on 3/4 in. long round head screws and are each provided with two washers as shown. The wheels revolve in recesses cut in the side plates which are made from 1/4 in. ply. The best way to make these plates is by cutting two

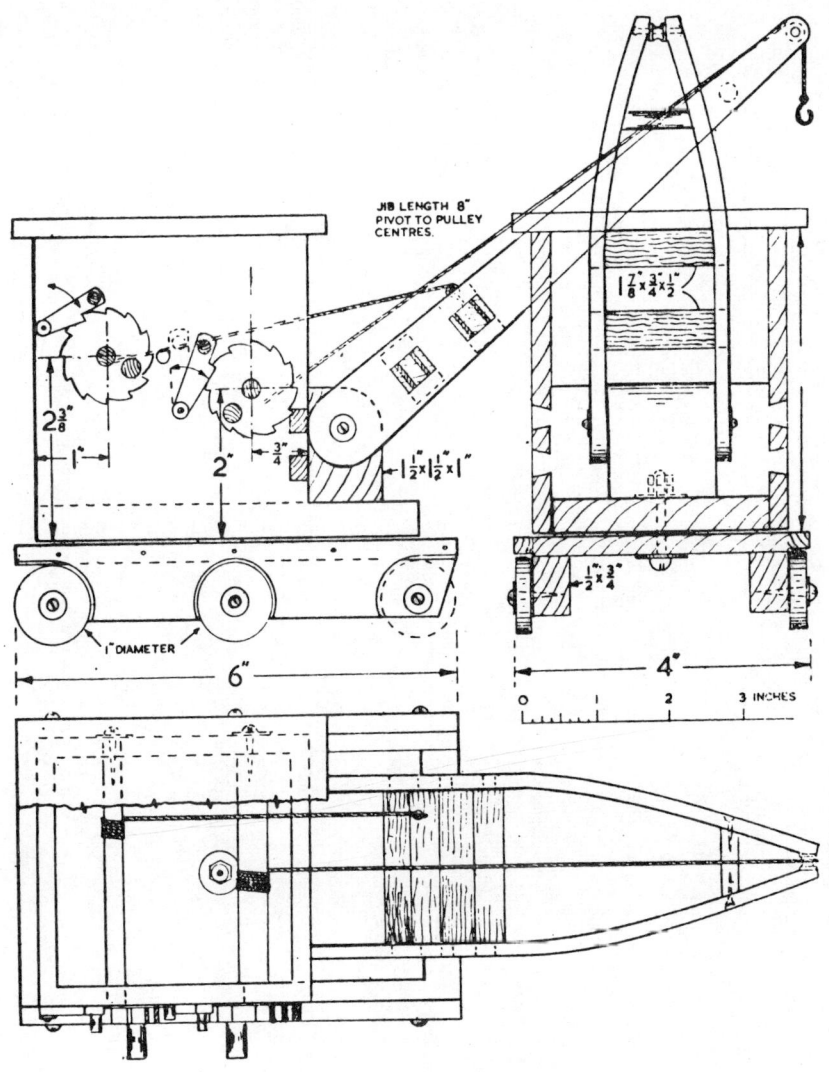

Fig. 18. Mobile Crane

strips of ply measuring 6.1/2 in. × 1.1/2 in. and boring each one with three 1.1/8 in. diameter holes. The waste can then be sawn and trimmed away and the plates mounted by pinning them to the sides of the bogie platform and the wheel battens.

The base of the cabin is a piece of hardwood measuring 5.1/4 in. × 3 in. × 3/8 in. and is pivoted on a 1/4 in. diameter metal screw. A large washer is placed between the cabin base and the bogie platform and a washer, nut and lock nut is used at the upper end.

The cabin is made up in 1/4 in. ply. The front and back are dovetailed into the sides which project to fit over the base and are screwed in position. The roof is cut with 1/4 in. overlap all round and is pinned in place. The pivot block for the jib is cut from hardwood and is glued in position. Screws driven through the base and the cabin front reinforce the joint.

To make a robust job which will stand hard use, the jib sides are cut from 1 in. by 3/16 in. hardwood tapering from 1 in. wide at the lower end, to 3/8 in. wide at the top. Two 3/4 in. × 1/2 in. struts are placed just in front of the pivot block and are wedge-tenoned to the sides of the jib. These hold the lower part of the jib firm and allow the sides to be sprung together without stressing the pivots. A short length of 1/4 in. dowel rod is used as a strut at the top end of the jib and is fixed with small screws driven through the sides. The pulley is a small wheel taken from a curtain runner and pivoted on brass wire. This is turned over at each end to prevent it working out. The jib itself is pivoted on screws and washers and the middle strut is fitted with a small screw eye to which the jib-cord is attached.

A pair of 1.1/4 in. diameter plain wooden wheels are used to make the ratchets for the winding gear. The central holes are opened out to 1/4 in. diameter and a 3/16 in. hole is bored in each wheel to accommodate the dowel rod handle which is glued in place. The actual cutting for the ratchets is not a difficult job to do provided it is tackled in a methodical manner. The easiest way is to draw the profile on thin cardboard which is then cut to shape and used as a template when marking the wheels. A fine dovetail saw or a light brass-backed saw is used for cutting the teeth and the waste is pared away with a bevel edged chisel. The cord shafts are cut from dowel rod, the jib-cord shaft being 1/4 in. in diameter, whilst the other is 3/8 in. reduced to 1/4 in. at each end. The two ratchets are glued to the ends of the shaft, the opposite ends being fixed with screws and washers as shown in Fig. 18. The two pawls are cut from 3/16 in. thick hardwood and are fitted with 1/8 in. dowel rod handles. They are pivoted on small round head screws and washers and should be quite free to move in and out of engagement with the ratchets. Macrama thread or thin twine is used for the cords. Notice that the jib cord is positioned to one side and therefore clear of the load bearing cord. Each is fixed by boring a small hole through the winding shaft through which the cords are threaded, the ends being knotted to prevent them pulling through. A small wire hook and a lead fishing weight are used on the load cord.

Chapter VI

TOYS FOR GIRLS

Doll's Wardrobe

All little girls like dressing and undressing their dolls and the wardrobe shown in Fig. 19 will be a welcome addition to their toys. The sides, top and base are cut from 3/8 in. thick hardwood and are rebated 1/4 in. wide by 1/4 in. deep at the rear edges to accommodate the 1/4 in. hardboard back. The top and bottom have stopped rebates 3/16 in. deep and 3/8 in. wide worked to receive the sides, thus forming half lap joints which are secured with glue and panel pins. The front edges are curved to correspond with the profile of the doors.

Inside the wardrobe is fixed a 3.1/2 in. wide by 1/4 in. thick hardboard shelf supported on small fillets pinned to the sides. A 1/4 in. diameter rod is let into sockets bored in the sides to act as a hanger rail.

The doors are made from 3/8 in. thick

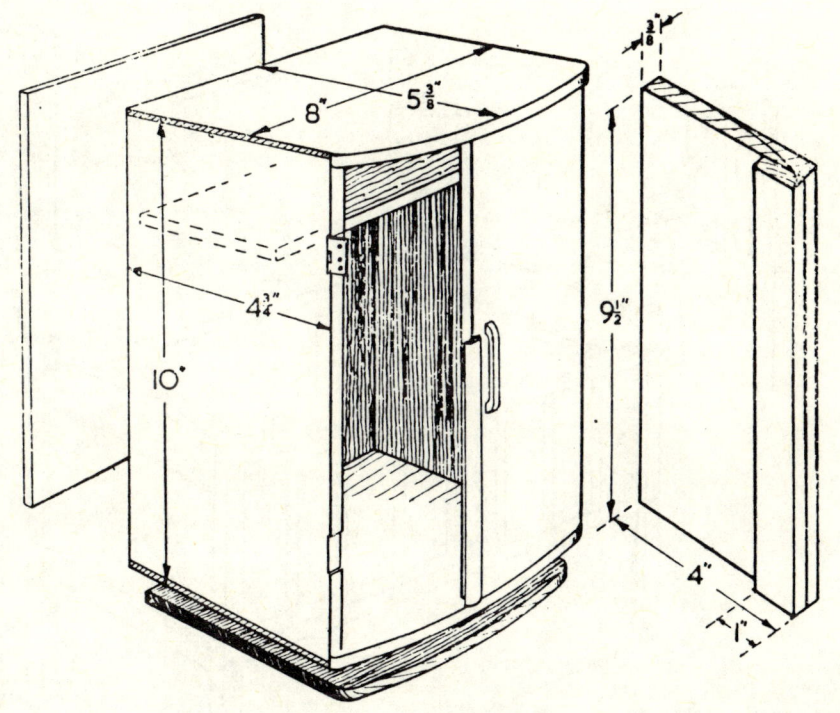

Fig. 19.   Doll's Wardrobe

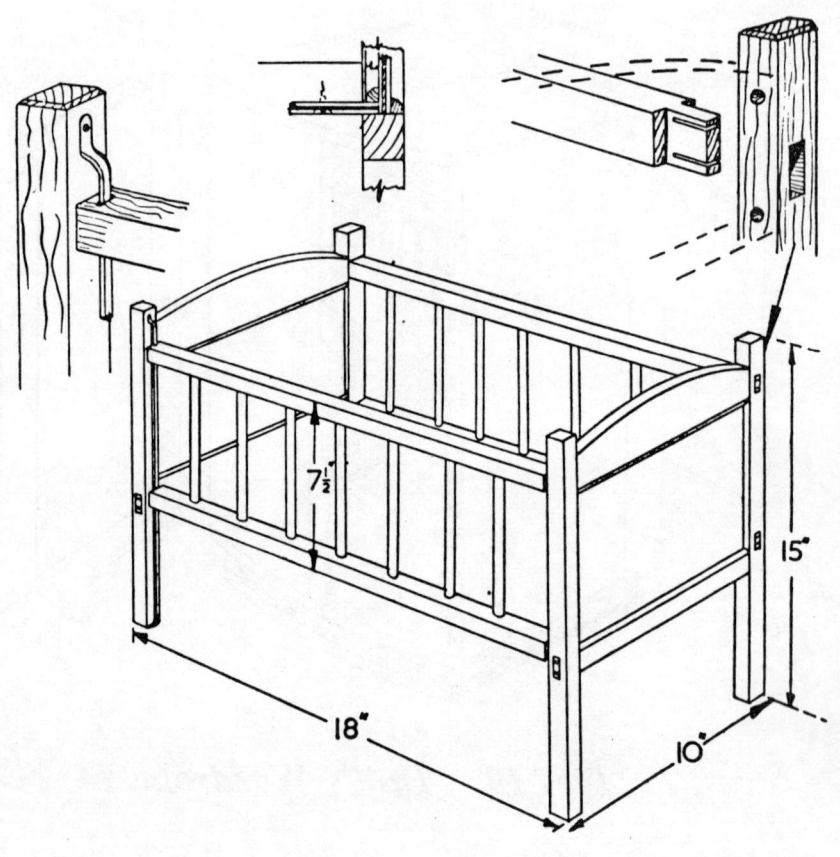

Fig. 20. *Doll's Cot*

hardwood, thickened at their hingeing edges with a 1 in. $\times$ 1/4 in. hardwood strip as shown in Fig. 19. This is glued in place and trimmed flush. The door profile is cut in cardboard which is used as a template when marking out. Plane away the waste and smooth with the scraper. To remove the last of the ridges, glasspaper wrapped round a cork block is used, working *across* the door faces.

Miniature brass butts are used to hinge the doors. They are let full thickness into the sides so as to ensure that the fixing screws do not come through the door fronts. A small ball catch is fixed in the top edge of each door and engages a striking plate let into the underside of the top. The right hand door has a strip of 1/2 in. half-round moulding glued to the face to cover the gap at the meeting edges. The handles can be bought ready made or cut from hardwood or plastic and fixed with small screws driven through the doors. The plinth is cut from 1/2 in. hardwood and is fixed with screws.

The best type of finish for this toy is undoubtedly paint or enamel and its appearance can be enhanced by fixing a pair of decorative transfers to each door.

Doll's Cot

This is a straightforward job to make in spite of its apparent complexity. The details are shown in Fig. 20. The work is started by making up the two ends. The legs and lower rail are 1 in. square battens put together with wedged mortise and tenon joints. The top rail is 2.1/4 in. × 1 in. stuff curved at the top edge and dowelled into the legs as shown inset Fig. 20. Notice that the dowel holes are bored so that they do not break into the mortises for the side framework rails. The 3/16 in. hardboard panels for the ends of the cot are held in place by 1/4 in. quarter-round mouldings which are pinned in place. These outer mouldings are pinned on but the remainder are not fixed until later.

The next job is to make up the fixed side from 1 in. square material and 3/16 in. diameter dowel rod. The rails are mortise and wedged into the legs. The lower side rail is placed so that its underside is 1/4 in. above the lower rail at the end of the cot. The cot base, which is supported on the end rails as shown inset Fig. 20, can then pass under the side rail to which it is screwed. This construction ensures a rigid job which will stand up to a good deal of hard wear. The seven uprights are fitted loosely into 3/16 in. diameter sockets bored 5/8 in. in or so deep into the top and bottom side rails.

Glue and cramp the joints, then cut and fit the 1/4 in. thick cot base. The end panels can next be fitted in place and secured by their mouldings.

The drop side is made up from 1 in. square stuff and 3/16 in. dowel rods. These are glued into their sockets and the two end uprights (which are 1 in. square material) — are mortise and tenoned to the rails. These two end uprights are necessary to ensure rigidity of the framework. The whole frame slides up and down on two lengths of brass curtain pelmet rail and slots are cut to accommodate these in the ends of the rails. The brass is easily bent and is drilled for small countersunk screws which hold the ends into shallow recesses cut in the legs. At the bottom, these recesses are formed underneath the leg, the rails being bent at right angles and secured with screws in the same way as at the top. To make sure that the drop-side will slide easily on its runners, a little melted candle wax is run into the slots in the rails to act as a lubricant.

Toy Dresser

This type of toy fascinates little girls and whilst a fair amount of work is involved in its making, the pleasure it brings the youngster is ample repayment. Enamelled in bright colours it will look most attractive.

The construction views are given in Fig. 21 and 3/8 in. ply is the most suitable material to use for the main parts. The various grooves are easily cut by sawing down the sides and stripping away two or more plies as needed to reach the required depth.

Cut the sides, top and bottom to shape and work 1/4 in. by 1/4 in. rebates along the back edges to receive the 1/4 in. ply or hardboard back, which is fixed in place with panel pins. The sides are dovetailed to the top and bottom, the *dovetails* being cut in the sides and the *sockets* in the top and bottom.

Parts A, B, C and D (Fig. 21), are all 3/8 in. ply and are housed into the sides. They are fitted dry and held with panel pins driven through the outside. The table top (Part B) is widened at the front and is pinned down on to the sides. The sliding flap is also cut from 3/8 in. ply, the shape being indicated at the inset view. To prevent this

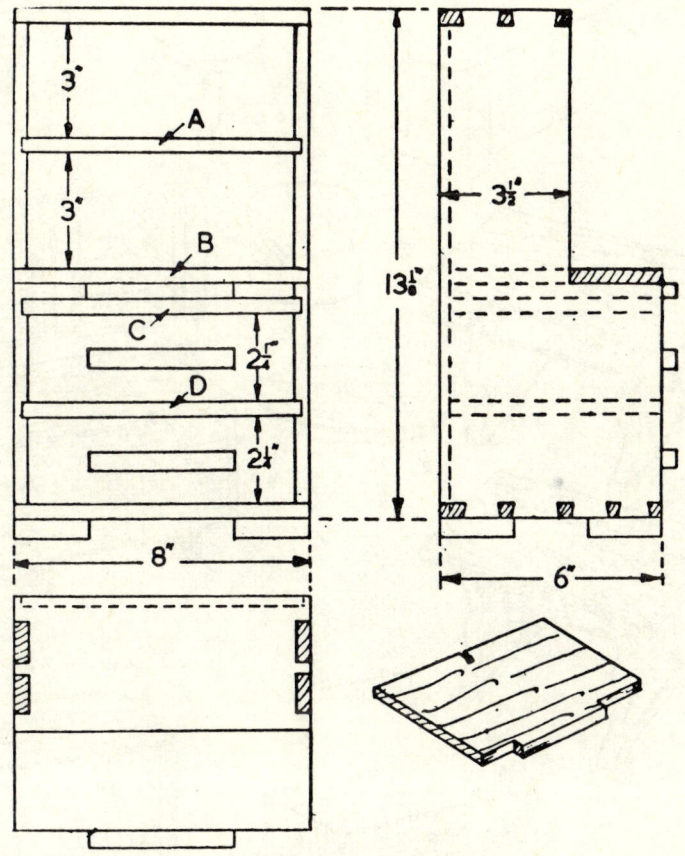

Fig. 21.   Doll's Dresser

Fig. 22.   Doll's Furniture

being pulled right out, a small hole is bored as shown and is countersunk on the underside. At the top, a small channel is gouged and a short length of cord is knotted and the free end passed up through the hole. This cord passes through a hole drilled in the back and is knotted to prevent it pulling through. It limits the amount by which the flap can be pulled out and should be adjusted so that not more than two thirds of the flap can be exposed.

The drawer construction is of the simplest type, plain lap joints being used throughout. The fronts are in 3/8 in. ply whilst the sides and back are 1/4 in. ply. The bottoms are best in 3/16 in. hardboard. All the joints are secured with panel pins and the heads are punched in. The four corner blocks for the plinth are cut from 1/2 in. hardwood and are glued in place.

When finishing this toy the grain should be well filled and glasspapered smooth. A couple of undercoats may be necessary if the wood is absorbent. The insides of the drawers can be enamelled if desired but their outer surfaces should be left plain, or they will certainly stick in the carcase.

Doll's Furniture

This class of toy is always popular with little girls, whether they possess a doll's house or not. It can be made from scraps and with the aid of a little ingenuity some most attractive items are easily contrived. Fig. 22 shows a selection of pieces, others will no doubt come immediately to mind. The scope of these toys is almost endless, in fact any item of furniture which can be simplified and made in miniature form will be acceptable to the youngster.

It is, however, necessary to make the toys sufficiently robust to withstand the usage they will be subjected to and for this reason certain proportions observed in full scale furniture must be varied. For instance, chair legs would hardly stand any use if made in normal proportions and are therefore deliberately made thicker. Special care must also be taken to ensure that the glued joints are really secure and accurate cutting is therefore all the more important. Somehow, when making toy furniture, a number of workers neglect this essential fact with the result that the items come to pieces after very little use and with consequent disappointment to the child.

An important factor to consider in connection

with toy furniture is the upholstery. Little girls are surprisingly observant — and critical — of anything connected with textiles and the materials used for covering the upholstered types of furniture must be chosen with care. For instance, the settee shown in Fig. 22, covered with a scrap of velvet will be much more appreciated than if linen or even a brightly patterned cotton material is used. The average child's tastes and perceptions in this field are remarkably clear cut. A little thought given to the matter will not only increase the pleasure obtained from the toy, but may well lay the foundation for a sound aesthetic appreciation in later years. Here, then, are some notes about the toys.

Settee

Cut the parts from hardwood and cover the seat and back before fixing them together with panel pins. The inner surfaces of the sides are covered and the material is temporarily tacked round the edge of the blocks with gimp pins. The sides are then fixed by screwing through into the seat and back. The outer surfaces are then covered, the material being folded round the edges over the "inner" covering and is tacked off with gimp pins. A strip of velvet ribbon is stretched round the edges of the sides and is tacked off underneath with gimp pins. Four brass headed chair nails are used as castors.

Arm-chairs
These are made in exactly the same way as the settee.

Dining Chairs
The seats are wooden discs and have four holes bored in them to receive the legs. These are cut from 1/8 in. dowel rod and are tapered towards the foot. The easiest way to do this job is to fix a hand drill in the vice and insert the leg in the chuck. By turning the handle and employing a flat stick wrapped with glasspaper in the manner of a file, the taper can be quickly and smoothly produced.

The curved backs are made from two strips of veneer which are bent round a rod such as a broom handle and glued together. Lap them with tape and leave until thoroughly dry. (The rod must, of course, be the same diameter as the chair seat, in fact the seats themselves can be cut from the actual rod used for bending the former.)

Final shaping of the chair backs is done with a sharp knife or they may be cut out with a fret saw. A bevel is worked on the seat rim to obtain the slope of the back and this job is best done with a file. The slightly rough surface left by the file will assist the glue to hold when the back is set in place. Really strong adhesive such as Rawlplug "Durofix" or a casein cement are the best types to use. "Durofix" is also an excellent cement to use for fixing the circular scrap of velvet used to upholster the seat.

Dressing Stool

The seat of this item is cut from hardwood, the curves being gouged to shape and smoothed with No. 1 glasspaper. Tapered legs made from 1/8 in. dowel rod are glued into holes bored in the seat. Velvet or felt are suitable materials for the upholstery. The top is stuck on with "Durofix" and laps over the edges. A narrow strip of the same material as the top is fixed round the edges with small brass pins.

Pouffe

This very simply made toy is merely a miniature size cotton reel wrapped with cotton wool and covered with material. A length of embroidery silk or a strand from a discarded dressing-gown is used as a tie for the item.

Dining Table

This is made from the thin wood strips used for model aircraft construction, or, alternatively, the very thin (2 mm.) ply sometimes available as offcuts. Strips of wood for model aeroplane spars are used for the feet. The leg slab shaping is done with a really sharp knife, a suitable tool being the "X-acto" knife which has a large variety of interchangeable blades and is manufactured by Trix Ltd., 11, Old Burlington Street, London, W.1.

To smooth the edges and obtain the final shape, use a small diameter dowel rod wrapped with grade "o" glasspaper. The lower ends of the slab legs are tenoned into the feet, the mortises being cut with the knife and the joint glued. The strut is also cut out with the knife and is tenoned into the slab ends. The tenons protrude and are glued and wedged with tiny pieces of dowel. The top is made in four pieces as indicated in Fig. 22, the upper ends of the slab legs being glued into the housings formed by the three underlinings of the top.

Stain and spirit varnish are suitable finishes for this item.

Sideboard

Also made from model aeroplane material, this item is glued and assembled with veneer pins. The sides are thickened at the front and back with strips of spare material. The front corners are rounded with glasspaper whilst the back strips are set in to form a rebate in which the back itself can be glued.

The top and base are glued on and a veneer pin is used at each corner to reinforce the joint. The central strut is also glued and reinforced with veneer pins. Notice how this is made from two pieces, the front one being from the same material used for the doors. The latter are thickened at their hingeing edges and rounded with glasspaper. Veneer pins are used as pivots and are driven through the top and base. Two scraps of spar material are used for handles and are glued on. The plinths are merely solid blocks glued in place.

Wardrobe

Constructed in a similar manner to the sideboard, this toy uses only a single door. It is pivoted on veneer pins driven through the base and top and shuts against a rebate formed by glueing an extra thickness strip at the closing edge.

Dressing Table

The sides of this item are cut from 3/16 in. ply which is grooved 1/8 in. wide and 1/8 in. deep (the thickness of two plies) for the shelf. This is in thin "aeroplane model" wood and is glued into the grooves to give the item rigidity. The front edge of each side is then lipped with a strip of wood and is rounded with glasspaper.

The top and base are in 1/8 in. wood fixed by glueing in place, the back also is 1/8 in. thick and is glued on. The drawer construction is quite simple but needs accurate marking and cutting. The front and back are 3/16 in. ply rebated for the 1/8 in. thick sides and base. No pins are used for fixing, the joints relying on the glue. Suitable adhesives are casein cement or Rawlplug "Durofix".

The mirror is a small handbag "replacement"

mirror cemented with "Durofix" to two shaped pillars which are glued to the back of the model. Two wood blocks are glued on to serve as plinths.

Coffee Table

A very easily constructed toy, this consists of a wooden disc in which four tapered legs are glued (on the same principle as the dining chair), and a top cut from 2 mm. ply glued in place.

Chapter VII

LARGE TOYS

THE following toys have been grouped together irrespective of their prevalent use by boys or girls. Where metal parts such as wheels, brackets, etc., are used, these should always be obtained before starting to construct the toy. For this reason such points as the diameter of axles or bolt holes will of course be dependent upon the actual item and may possibly vary from the dimensions shown in the following drawings.

Scooter

Shown in Fig. 23, this toy is quite easy to construct. It is important that only sound timber, that is to say timber free from knots, splits and pests, is used. All the parts are cut from 1 in. thick material. The front is slotted for the wheel and bored to take the axle. This would be a coach bolt about 5 in. long and 3/8 in. or 1/2 in. diameter. The head has a square part which is let into the wood and steel washers are used each side of the wheel. Two nuts are used, the outer one acting as a lock nut. If the thread of the bolt projects beyond the lock nut, it should be cut off with a hack saw and the burrs filed away.

The upper part of the handle is bowsawn to shape and smoothed with a round faced spokeshave. A slight chamfer is worked on all edges to make sure that there are no dead square corners on which the child may come to harm. The handle is also cut from 1 in. thick material and a wedged mortise and tenon joint is used. The rounding of the handle grips is of course done with a spokeshave and is finished with glasspaper.

The footboard is slotted for the rear wheel which is fixed in the same manner as the front one. The pivot block is cut to shape and a bridle joint is used between this and the footboard. Casein glue is used and the joint is reinforced with a couple of 3/8 in. dowel rods which pass right through the footboard and are glued in place.

To pivot the front of the scooter, a pair of metal brackets are used as shown in Fig. 23. The brackets are identical in size and are fixed in place with round head steel screws. A 3/8 in. bolt

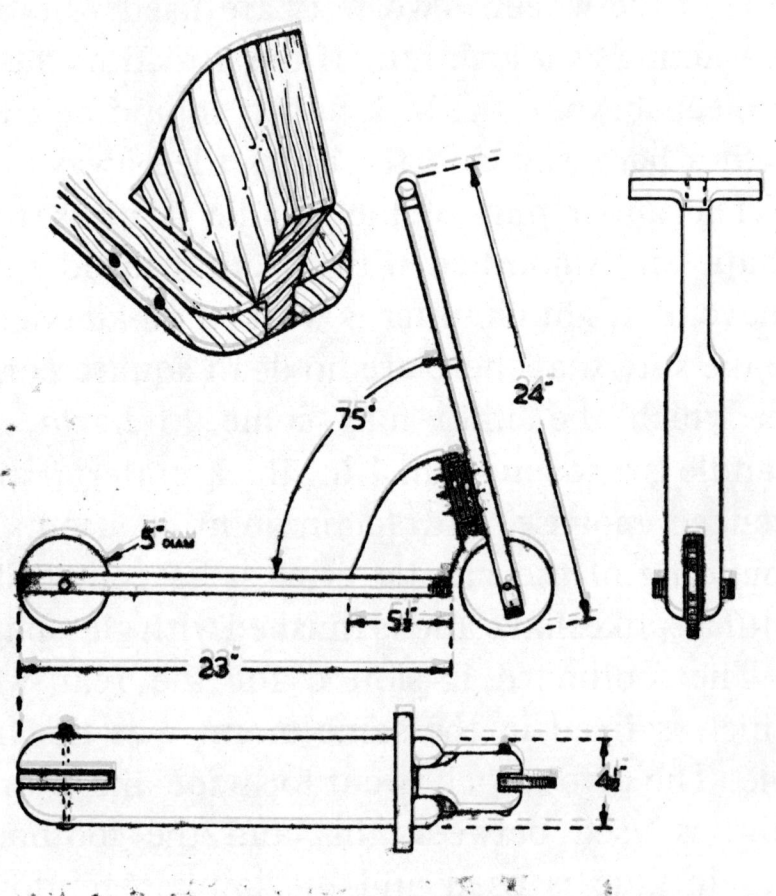

Fig. 23. Scooter

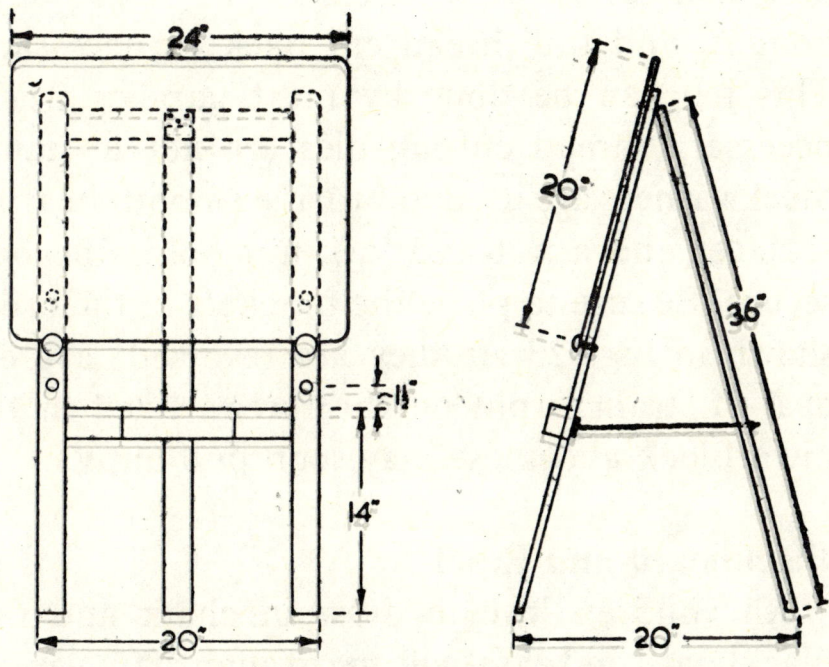

Fig. 24. Blackboard

is used as the actual pivot and the length must be selected so that the brackets bear on the plain shank of the bolt. This may mean that a longer bolt than is actually needed will have to be bought, and the thread cut back as necessary. This job can be done by most garages if the necessary thread cutting dies are not to hand. Steel washers are used to provide smooth bearing surfaces and a nut and lock-nut holds the bolt secure. Be sure to place the brackets in the order shown in Fig. 23. If they are reversed, a great deal of strain is put on the screws fixed in the pivot block and these may soon pull away.

Blackboard and Easel

All children love to draw in chalk and this blackboard and easel will guard against unwanted "decorations" appearing on the room walls! The main framework of the easel is made up in 2 in. by 7/8 in. hardwood, the braces being in the same material, mortise and tenoned in place. The two uprights each measure 37 in. long, the upper brace being set 1 in. from the ends. A shallow chalkbox made from 1/4 in. ply through dovetailed at the corners is screwed to the lower brace and holes are bored in the uprights for the adjusting pegs. They are spaced at 2 in. centres, the lower ones being 1.1/2 in. above the brace as shown in Fig. 24.

The rear leg is cut from 2 in. by 7/8 in. hardwood and is fixed to the top brace with a large hinge. To restrict the amount of opening, a hardwood block is bored with a 1/4 in. diameter hole and recessed at the front. A cord is knotted and passed through the hole in this block, which is then screwed to the lower brace. The knot, of course, rests in the recess. The other end of the cord passes through a hole bored in the rear leg and is knotted at the required distance.

The blackboard itself is cut from 1/4 in. ply or hardboard, the edges and corners being rounded and smoothed with glasspaper. A coat of black spirit stain is applied to blacken the board.

The adjustment pegs can be small wooden drawer handles which are made with a shank, intended to be glued into holes bored in the drawer front. The shanks are glasspapered smooth and reduced to make an easy fit in the holes bored in the front uprights.

Doll's Pram

Although at first sight this toy appears to be a

complicated item to make, the construction is, in fact, perfectly straightforward. Fig. 25 shows the constructional view and the first job is to make a full-scale drawing of the item which will be used to obtain the body profile template and to check the positions of various parts.

Side Frames

The sides of the pram consist of a framework of 5/8 in. thick hardwood covered with thin ply. The framework is half lap jointed together and the first step is to prepare the horizontal members to length and width. The top members measure 21 in. $\times$ 1.1/2 in. $\times$ 5/8 in. and the lower ones are 17 in. $\times$ 2.1/2 in. $\times$ 5/8 in. The four sloping members are each 12 in. $\times$ 3.1/2 in. $\times$ 5/8 in. and the angle at which they are placed is not critical, provided a reasonable area is allowed for the half lap joints.

The half laps are marked and cut in the horizontal members first. To do this, lay the two pieces on the full scale drawing, then place the sloping members in position. The angle of the half laps is then marked in pencil on the horizontal parts and can then be cut over with the knife. The depth of the joint is gauged in and the

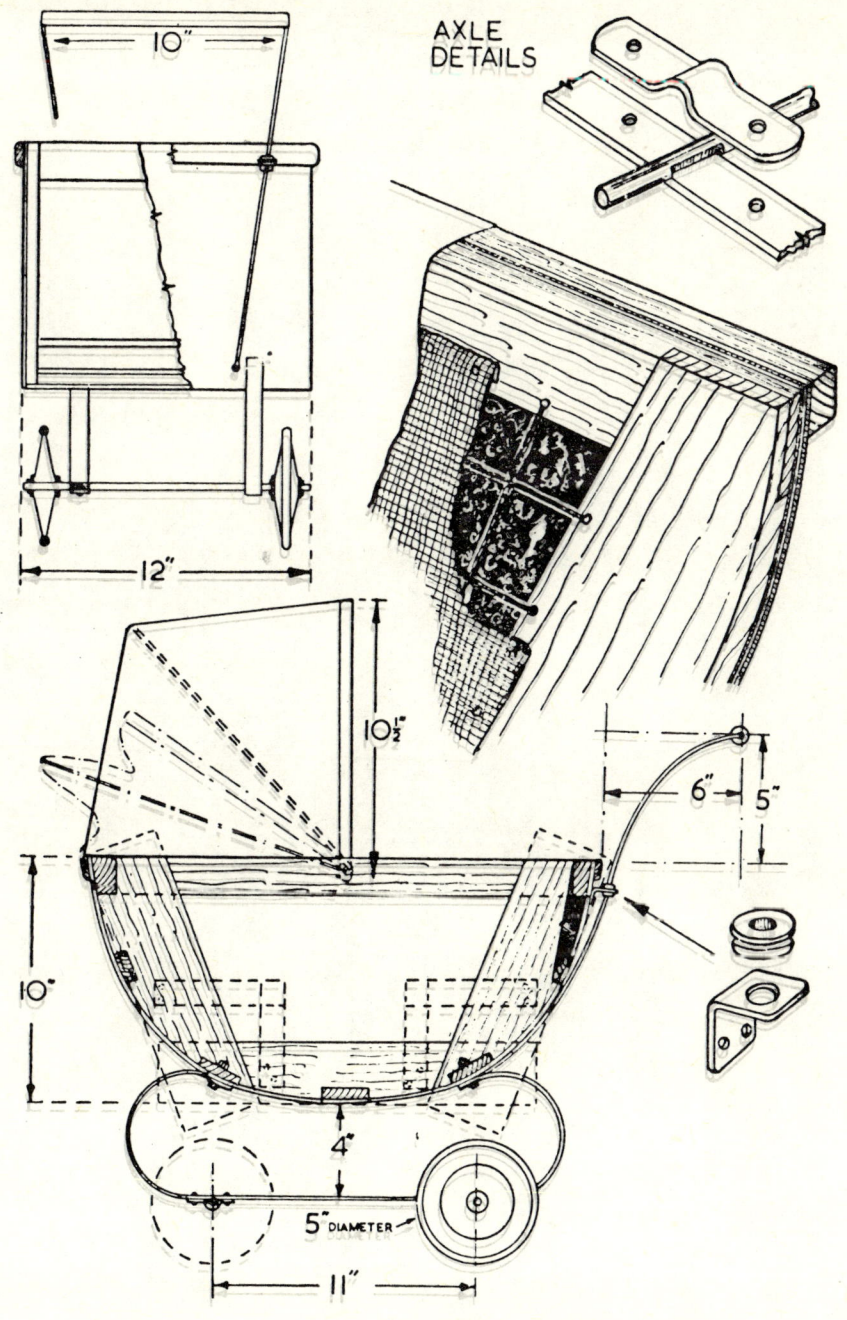

AXLE
DETAILS

10"

12"

10½"

10"

6"

5"

4"

5" DIAMETER

11"

Fig. 25.   Doll's Pram

waste sawn away. A small block plane is used to trim the joint. To make the other halves of the joints, the sloping members are laid on the full-scale drawing and the horizontal ones placed "upside down" over them. See that the sloping members butt closely against the shoulders of the half-lap joints and mark the joint angles as before. Cut over, gauge the depth of the lap and complete the joints. The frameworks are then glued and cramped. When dry, they are laid on the bench and a cardboard template, obtained by tracing from the full-scale drawing, is used when marking in the profile. The waste is cut away with a bowsaw and the frames are trimmed back to profile with a spokeshave.

Braces

Six braces are used and care should be taken to see that they are all of equal length. They are all fixed by screwing through the side frames before the outer covering is put on. The top braces are 1.1/2 in. $\times$ 3/4 in. hardwood and are left square on their outer faces. All the others are convex on their outer faces to agree with the side frame profile. The shaping is done after the braces are fixed in place and they are positioned so that the centres of their outer faces register on the profile lines. The protruding corners are planed away and the brace reduced to profile.

Panels

The panels are cut from 3/16 in. or thinner plywood and are glued and pinned in place. The long curved panel should if possible be cut in one piece arranged so that the grain of the outer plies lies across the panel. If this cannot be managed, two separate pieces could be used, the butt joint between them being arranged under the central batten. A "cold" glue such as casein cement is the best to use and the panel is laid on the upturned carcase and pinned to the central batten. One side is then bent and pinned as far as the "axle" braces, then the other side is fixed as far as the "three quarter" braces. The original half is then finally bent and pinned, followed by the other end. In this way the panel is gradually bent and will lie closely against the framework profiles. If the work is started from one end there is a danger of pulling away the pins as the leverage is developed on bending the panel. Allow the glue to dry, then clean off any overlap.

The side panels are cut to shape, allowing a

small overlap all round. Coat the frameworks with glue and pin the panels into place. When dry clean away the overlap.

Seats

These are made from hardboard or plywood fixed to half-lap jointed supports as shown in Fig. 25, elevation and inset views. These supports are in 1 in. × 3/4 in. hardwood and are screwed to the side frames.

Upholstery

The pram is lined with leathercloth and the upholstery details are given in Fig. 25. Starting with the side panels, the centre is filled with flock or wadding and kept in place with a piece of scrim or hessian tacked to the framework. A few large stitches are run both ways across the hessian, using thin twine and an upholstery needle. These stitches catch the wadding and prevent it packing down into the well of the pram. The ends are treated in the same way, the hessian being tacked to the top and "three quarter" braces.

The leathercloth is cut slightly larger than required and the work of attaching it to the pram is started with the sides. Lay the pram on one side and place the leathercloth reverse face up on the side of the body. See that the top edge of the material is about 1/4 in. below the edge of the pram side, then screw on the batten. Bring the cloth over the batten and stretch it down smoothly. Tack off to the side framework, doubling the edge under and tacking through the two thicknesses. Where the edge shows, that is, in the seat well, use short upholstery chair nails instead of tacks. The material is folded under and "mitred" at the end of the battens. The ends are covered in the same way, the material being tacked off to the "three-quarter" battens. Short fillets of 1/2 in. × 1/2 in. stuff tacked to the side frames between the tope and "three-quarter" braces enable the material to be tacked off neatly after having the edges folded under. Chair nails should be used at this position.

Undercarriage

The springs are bent from strip iron or mild steel about 3/4 in. wide by 1/16 in. or so thick. It is bent cold by hammering over a fairly large diameter block of wood. Each spring should be checked for shape against the full-scale drawing and it is important that both springs should be alike. At their tops, the springs are bolted to the carriage braces as shown in Fig. 25. The axles are mild steel and their diameters will of course be governed by the wheel axle holes. This is usually of the order of 1/4 in. to 3/8 in. for 5 in. diameter wheels but should be checked before ordering the material. To secure the axles to the springs, "flats" are filed as shown inset Fig. 25, and metal clips are bent from a scrap of the spring material and riveted into place. The "flats" are to prevent the axle from turning. When placing the clips it is very important to check that the axles will lie square with the springs and parallel to each other. Unless this is so, the pram will tend to run to one side.

Handle

The handle is a length of 3/4 in. diameter hardwood dowel rod and is supported on two lengths of 3/16 in. diameter mild steel rod. Two metal brackets bored with holes to take rubber grommets, are screwed to the top braces and hold the handle supports in place. The ends of the supports are heated and beaten flat. When cool they are trimmed with a smooth file and drilled for the fixing screws.

Hood

The front strip of the hood can be made from the same material as the undercarriage springs. A hem is stitched in the material and the metal is slipped into the "pocket" thus formed. The other hoop is bent from stout wire and is formed into a ring at each end for fixing purposes. To hold it in place with respect to the hood, a few tapes are stitched to the latter to form loops through which the wire passes. The material itself is fixed to the outside of the pram body with chair nails. The pivot for the hoops are wood screws which have a metal thread and a wing nut instead of the ordinary plain shank and head. Steel washers are used to increase the bearing surfaces and ensure that the hoops can be moved smoothly and yet be positively held in place.